To Michelle,
I hope you enjoy
decluttering!
With love
Fiona Cade

Living Simply

FIONA CASTLE
WITH
JAN GREENOUGH

David C Cook

transforming lives together

LIVING SIMPLY
Published by David C. Cook
Kingsway Communications LTD
Lottbridge Drove, Eastbourne BN23 6NT, England

David C. Cook
4050 Lee Vance View, Colorado Springs, CO 80918 U.S.A.

David C. Cook Distribution Canada
55 Woodslee Avenue, Paris, Ontario, Canada N3L 3E5

David C. Cook and the graphic circle C logo
are registered trademarks of Cook Communications Ministries.

Unless otherwise indicated, all Scripture quotations are taken from The
Touchpoint Bible (New Living Translation) © 1996 published by Tyndale House
Publishers, Wheaton, Illinois. Verses marked NIV are from the New International
Version © 1973, 1978, 1984 by the International Bible Society. Verses marked
NRSV are from the New Revised Standard Version, copyright © 1989 by the
Division of Christian Education of the National Council of the Churches of
Christ in the USA.

ISBN 978-1-84291-252-2

Printed in the United States of America
First Edition 2006

5 6 7 8 9 10

101510

Contents

Preface

This book grew out of a presentation I gave at a Christian event called 'Easter People'. The theme that year was 'Destiny', and I began thinking about what prevents us as Christians from pursuing our destiny.

Nothing is more important than finding and fulfilling God's purpose for us. Yet most of us have so much clutter in our lives that we can't make time and space to listen to him.

- Some of it is physical clutter – the masses of possessions that we accumulate.
- Some of it is emotional clutter – our baggage of hopes, fears and muddled relationships.
- Some of it is spiritual clutter – our assumptions, ambitions and attitudes.

As Christians we have to live in the world alongside our neighbours, and it's easy to get drawn into the ways of the world and to adopt its aspirations. It's good to do an audit and look not just at the belongings we've collected but also at the ideas, prejudices and priorities which may have crept in without our noticing. The things we collect around us can provide pointers to what is really important to us.

We can choose to clear out the clutter from our lives. It can set us free to hear from God, to realise our potential and achieve the destiny to which he calls us.

1

Passport to Peru

My daughter Julia spent eleven years living in a shanty town in Peru. She kept asking me to visit her, and eventually I gathered my courage and went. It was a life-changing experience. I had seen plenty of television documentaries and I thought I knew what to expect, but nothing could have prepared me for the reality: the sights, the smells, the sounds – and the grinding poverty.

Julia herself was living in a small shanty-town dwelling. Her cupboard was a pile of orange boxes lined with newspaper; her kitchen equipment consisted of two knives. Like all mothers, my first impulse was to give her things. 'Let me buy you a cupboard,' I said.

'Mum,' she replied, 'I have everything I need. I don't want to live any differently from my neighbours.'

We went to visit a village outside Lima, where she was teaching the women to make jewellery to earn money to feed their families. The journey itself was epic. First we took a white-knuckle ride in a *combi* (a dilapidated minibus), then at the foot of the mountain we changed to a *collectivo* (an old car with no bonnet, bald tyres and lots of us crammed onto seats with the springs poking out). Finally we got out and walked.

The church where Julia taught had no roof, only a piece of corrugated iron over the lectern. The women greeted us warmly and gave me a tremendous welcome as Julia's mother. After the lesson they prepared a simple meal of corn cut from the cob, pounded with cheese, wrapped in a corn leaf and boiled in water. A banquet at Buckingham Palace could not have been as special as this sacrificial meal. One woman gave me a little brooch she had made and pinned it onto my shirt, saying, 'We want to give you this because we love you. Please forgive us for the way we are.' I wanted her to forgive me for the way I was! I was overwhelmed by her kindness and affection.

These women had little in the way of possessions, but they were rich in love. They had no fancy homes to occupy them, so they spent time with other people. It made me wonder about our lavish Western lifestyles. We have so much materially, but along the way have we lost love, care and the ability to share? Today in the developed world we have more material belongings, more educational opportunities and more leisure time than ever before, yet it's doubtful whether any of these things make people happier. Instead, there is a growth industry of life coaches, happiness doctors, gurus and teachers all offering various routes to tranquillity. There are even television programmes about decluttering our homes, aimed at helping us to find peace by learning to manage the sheer volume of possessions we have accumulated.

Yet Jesus offers us everything we need. 'Peace I leave

with you; my peace I give you' (John 14:27 NIV). 'The fruit of the Spirit is love, joy, peace, patience, kindness, goodness, faithfulness, gentleness and self-control' (Galatians 5:22 NIV).

When I came home I resolved that I would clear out the clutter of my life. I wanted to be more wholehearted for God, to live more simply, and not to spend time and money on things that don't matter. I wasn't trying to copy the poverty-stricken people of Peru, lovely though they were. There would be no point in stepping right outside my own culture and living in a way that would be deemed utterly eccentric by all the people around me. I could go and live in a garden shed – but no one would take me seriously! I have to have something in common with people before they will listen to me, and if we are to preach the gospel effectively to our friends and neighbours we have to be accepted by them.

I wanted to be 'in the world but not of it', to face all the issues of modern life but not to share the values of materialism and selfishness that our culture promotes. I wanted to identify the places where I was being deflected from my primary purpose of living a life that was honouring God and leading people to know Jesus. It meant taking a hard look at my life, and I found the best way to start was to look at the place where I live.

Join me in a walk around our homes. You may not have all these rooms or all these possessions – maybe you live in a bedsit. But you can still benefit from the same exercise, examining what's important in your life. If you are hard up and struggling, remember that God can use a little to make much more. The prophet Elisha said to the widow, 'What do you have in the house?' and went on to fill her oil jars to overflowing (2 Kings 4:2–6). In fact, God seems to find it easier to use people who have a little (like the boy with five loaves and two small fish, Mark 6:22–44) than those who have a lot (like the rich young man, Mark 10:17–22).

It's so easy for us to become the prisoners of our possessions, so that our homes take over our lives. It's easy for us to slip into patterns of thinking and attitudes that are preoccupied with material things rather than spiritual ones.

> Do not store up treasures here on earth, where they can be eaten by moths and get rusty, and where thieves break in and steal. Store your treasures in heaven, where they will never become moth-eaten or rusty and where they will be safe from thieves. Wherever your treasure is, there your heart and thoughts will also be. (Matthew 6:19–21)

Let's examine ways of living more simply, so that we can simply live – in the way God wants us to.

The Front Door

2

The Baggage of Our Lives

The trouble tree

Do we allow the problems of our day to colour our mood when we get home? I once read a story about a man who hired a carpenter. On the first day of the job, everything went wrong: an important piece of equipment needed repair, the job turned out to be more complicated than expected, and at the end of it the carpenter's van broke down. The man offered to drive him home and the carpenter invited him in to meet his family. As they approached the front door, the man saw the carpenter do a strange thing. He went up to a small tree in the front garden and touched its lower branches with both hands. As he opened the front door, his whole manner changed. He stood taller, his face broke into a wide smile, he hugged his two small children and kissed his wife.

Afterwards, as they said goodbye at the door, the employer asked, 'What were you doing when we came in?'

'Oh, that's my trouble tree,' the workman replied. 'I can't

avoid having troubles at work, but they don't belong at home with the family. So I hang them up on the tree every night before I go in. Then in the morning I pick them up again. The funny thing is, when I come out in the morning there never seem to be as many as I remember leaving there the night before!'

It's so easy to allow the kind of day we've had to affect our behaviour with everyone else at home. Often we take out our frustrations on those closest to us, because they are more likely to put up with our behaviour. Some people work under conditions of great stress, and this makes them irritable when they get home as they give vent to the anger they have suppressed all day. Their families may find it hard to say anything that won't detonate an explosion. Others have demanding jobs, and this makes them so tired that they have no energy to do anything but collapse in a heap when they get home. What message does that send to a partner or children? 'My work is more important to me than you are.'

A mother with small children may be so tired when her husband gets home that she just wants him to take over the childcare for a while, and she forgets that he may need to unwind first. I remember someone saying once, 'You think your husband comes home at 7 p.m., but actually it's only his body that arrives then. The rest of him doesn't arrive till he's had his dinner and watched television for at least an hour!'

When my own children were small I deeply resented the advice given to wives in those days, that they should make themselves look attractive when their husband came home from work. But that was the 'pit' hour! I was exhausted from coping with four small children – often for many days at a time while Roy was working away from home. When he got back I knew he would be tired from travelling and looking forward to a loving welcome from the family he'd been missing, but all I could do was pour out all my problems, tell him how tired I was and how difficult the children had been, and complain that he was disturbing them when I'd just got them ready for bed. It wasn't until after I became a Christian that I learned how to deal with my own moods and pay attention to the power I had over the emotional tone of our family life.

Some of us find it especially hard to control our irritability or resentment, perhaps because of difficulties in our own upbringing. There may be baggage from our past that we bring into our homes and our marriages. We all have problems that we live with, but we don't have to continue to live with them and let them spoil the atmosphere for everyone else. As Christians we have access to the greatest helper of all, the Holy Spirit, the 'Comforter' (in the sense of giving strength), who can heal us and guide us in our daily struggles. 'The unfailing love of the LORD never ends. . .Great is his faithfulness; his mercies begin afresh each day' (Lamentations 3:22–23).

Do we really want to spoil the relationships that matter most to us – with our parents, husband, wife or children – because of our attitudes? By God's grace we can begin afresh every morning and leave behind whatever troubles we have. Let's think about that, and dump our troubles outside the front door when we go in, in order to be the person God wants us to be with our loved ones.

Trust me, I'm a Christian

It isn't just the cares of the day that we need to be able to cast aside. There are other items of baggage we carry about with us that also affect our relationships with friends and family and the work we do for God.

We know that as Christians we are ambassadors for Christ and that people look closely at our lives to see whether we live up to the ideals we preach. They are quick to detect any suspicion of hypocrisy and may regard the slightest failure as proof that 'all that faith business' doesn't work after all.

This puts us under great pressure. We don't want to let the Lord down, yet we are ordinary, fallible human beings, just like everyone else. We aim to be good, but often fail; we do some things we regret; we fail to do other things we ought to do. When this happens, we know we can always take our sins and shortcomings to our heavenly Father in repentance and receive his forgiveness – but are we as willing to acknowledge our failures to other people? Do we always tell the truth, scrupulously and fearlessly?

> Search me, O God, and know my heart;
> test me and know my thoughts.
> Point out anything in me that offends you,
> and lead me along the path of everlasting life.
> (Psalm 139:23–24)

It's very tempting to try to make excuses, to try to find alibis for our indiscretions. Sometimes we can hardly bear to acknowledge things to ourselves and attempt to place the blame elsewhere: 'I knew that conversation was turning into gossip, but the others would have been offended if I'd walked away.' 'Everyone else fiddles their expenses. If I don't do it too, they'll all be caught and it'll be my fault.'

Roy always used to say, 'The first time you tell a lie is the hardest; after that it gets easier.' However, lies need to be covered up and backed up, and we live in fear of being found out. This makes good, trusting relationships difficult to maintain. If you genuinely forgot to go to a meeting (or even if you simply didn't want to go), it's better to say so rather than make up a story about an emergency that prevented you from being there. So what if you have to admit to being absent-minded, or to having other priorities? Sometimes our self-esteem is so fragile that we can't face people knowing that we sometimes make mistakes. Yet cheating or lying about our lives makes us less than the honest, honourable and faithful people God requires us to be. 'Instead, we will speak the truth in love, growing in every way more and more like Christ' (Ephesians 4:15).

> *'Although God loves us as we are, he loves us too much to let us stay as we are.'*
>
> *Selwyn Hughes*

Who, me?

We all have prejudices. 'Who, me?' I hear you say. 'I'm not a racist. I don't mind encountering different cultures.' We always assume that prejudice is racial, cultural or religious, yet there are many different kinds of prejudice. We may have fixed ideas about our roles at work or at church. 'Oh, I could never do that,' we say. We cling to particular styles of worship, or allow ourselves to become preoccupied with the business of running a church, rather than focusing on the real purpose of Christian fellowship.

Think back to last Sunday's church service. Who was leading the worship? Did you wish it was someone else? Was the worship too loud, too quiet, too modern, too traditional, too long, too short, too popular or too theological for you? And did the person sitting next to you have a different opinion? Were they wrong?

Some of our opinions are very firmly held. We always deny being prejudiced, but we do think that we're right.

> *'Around 90 per cent of the entire work force and resources in the church . . . are used for maintenance. Less than 10 per cent is used for mission.'*
>
> *J. John*

I once went to a church meeting where we spent almost the whole time discussing the colour of the new carpet. We eventually came to a decision. Someone got the colour they wanted – but when they get to heaven I somehow can't imagine God taking them to one side and saying, 'I'm so glad you decided on blue. I didn't like the thought of you having a red carpet.' Who cares? It'll be worn out in a few years, anyway. We spend so much time worrying about peripheral things that have no eternal value.

Let's think about what's really important. There's a world out there, dying without Christ, while we waste our time on matters of church organisation. There are people without a roof over their heads, and we worry about the housekeeping and decoration in our churches.

If we are really open to God, we will be prepared to set aside our prejudices and opinions, and we will be ready to seek out and do God's will, whether or not it's something we have ever considered before. Tony Campolo, the sociologist and Baptist minister, says, 'Life for most of us is a constant struggle in which we never stop considering what it is we should become. In dialogue with God, we need to establish what we believe are viable missions, and set out to realise them. But each step along the way we must be ready to let go of the plans that have given our lives direction up until that point, and accept new challenges that might grow out of the dialogue.'

In Acts we read the story of how God took a dramatic step to challenge Peter's firmly held views.

The next day as Cornelius's messengers were nearing the city, Peter went up to the flat roof to pray. It was about noon, and he was hungry. But while lunch was being prepared, he fell into a trance. He saw the sky open, and something like a large sheet was let down by its four corners. In the sheet were all sorts of animals, reptiles, and birds. Then a voice said to him, 'Get up, Peter; kill and eat them.'

'Never, Lord,' Peter declared. 'I have never in all my life eaten anything forbidden by our Jewish laws.'

Then the voice spoke again, 'If God says something is acceptable, don't say it isn't.' The same vision was repeated three times. Then the sheet was pulled up again to heaven.

Peter was very perplexed. What could the vision mean? Just then the men sent by Cornelius found the house and stood outside at the gate. They asked if this was the place where

Simon Peter was staying. Meanwhile, as Peter was puzzling over the vision, the Holy Spirit said to him, 'Three men have come looking for you. Go down and go with them without hesitation. All is well, for I have sent them.' (Acts 10:9–20)

God had to challenge Peter's thinking, because he was still stuck in the old ways of Jewish traditions, which forbade him to eat certain foods or go into the homes of Gentiles. He had not yet understood that Jesus had changed everything by his life and death, and that the gospel was for everyone, rich and poor, male and female, Jew and Gentile. God knew that Peter could never reach other people while his view of the world was limited by his prejudices, even though those prejudices were based on views which were once totally right! As soon as he was freed from those prejudices, God was able to use him. He then sent him miles away to meet one person, a Roman army officer, but as a result a whole group of people were converted.

It's worth looking at the process of that change in Peter: first he prayed, then he listened, and his mind was opened to a new idea. At first he rejected it ('Never, Lord'), but he was open to the prompting of the Holy Spirit and then he obeyed 'without hesitation'. He didn't think about the cost, or the sacrifice, or the consequences. He just went willingly to do what God wanted. Peter was willing to abandon his prejudices and step out in faith. We must be willing to keep listening to God, and be prepared to do things differently. Stepping out of our 'comfort zone' can be immensely rewarding if it frees us to find God's will for us. We don't have to feel threatened by change. God can use it to lead us along new paths of obedience to him.

Prayer

Father, please forgive me for all the times I have failed you – by inflicting my moods on other people, by being less than honest in facing up to my own behaviour, or by clinging to the safety of my own comfort zone.

Give me, I pray, the strength of the Holy Spirit to control my words and actions; the light of the Holy Spirit to see myself more clearly; and the power of the Holy Spirit so that I may have the courage to step out in faith to do your will. Amen.

The Hall

3

Setting Priorities

The hall is the gateway to the home, and we try to make it welcoming for family and friends. It helps if there isn't an obstacle course of discarded shoes and bags on the floor; if there isn't a pile of junk mail on the table; and if the hooks aren't full of so many old coats that there isn't room to hang up a visitor's jacket.

Making a pleasant and welcoming environment is important, but it's a good idea to look at how much time we spend on *things* rather than on people.

> *'Don't love anything that can't love you back.'*
> *Don Aslett*

The duplicating duck

Have you got collections of things? I was once given a china duck. It was yellow with a blue bow round its neck, and I put it on the window ledge in the downstairs loo. People saw it and they must have thought, 'Fiona's got a duck. I'll give her another one,' and before I knew it I had about six of them. They were growing into a collection. I'm absolutely certain that when I die and my children have to clear out the house, they'll sweep them all into a box with great glee and send them straight to the next jumble sale. But meanwhile I dutifully dust them, because that's what you do!

Collections of things take time. You have to dust and clean them, and sometimes you buy special shelves and display cabinets for them. They demand bits of your time and money and attention, often for very little return. Watch out for duplicating ducks.

Looking after our homes means dusting, polishing, cleaning, painting and renovating. It's like painting the Forth Bridge – it never stops, and it all takes up time and energy. It's important that we do it (if you don't, you end up on one of those *other* television programmes which specialise in dirty houses!), but how do we find the right balance in our lives?

Learn to delegate

Finding out what we should be spending our time on may be a question of asking ourselves what we're good at and focusing on that. Find out, too, which things you're not so good at and learn to delegate them. It gives other people a chance to try out new activities and an opportunity to shine. That way we're all learning and working together.

The young church discovered this principle early on. They had organised a daily distribution of food, but the system was falling apart. The apostles realised that there was too much for twelve men to do and they said, 'It would not be right for us to neglect the ministry of the word of God in order to wait on tables' (Acts 6:2 NIV). They chose seven others and turned the responsibility over to them.

Examine yourself and find out where your efforts are best used. Don't deceive yourself with false modesty (there's never any point in pretending to God), but be honest. It may be that you have exactly the right gifts to wait on tables and be a blessing to everyone you serve. But use your talents wisely. We need to think about where we can be most valuable.

I once met a woman who had two children, a busy husband, a large house and a full-time job as a GP. She also had a cleaning lady. Everyone was very happy with the arrangement, until someone began to criticise. Wasn't she ashamed to make someone else clean up her mess? Shouldn't she be at home (even though her children were at school all day) cleaning her own kitchen floor? She spent a great deal of time worrying about this, until one day she mentioned it to the cleaning lady, who was blessed with rather more common sense.

'Well, if you didn't employ me, I'd be out of a job and short of money,' she said. 'And anyway, it's a much better use of your time to be looking after people when they're ill. You do that very well, but I happen to know that you clean floors rather badly.'

What's important?

Of course, this is about much more than just cleaning. If you thought that today was going to be the last day of your life, how many of the routine jobs would you bother with?

You wouldn't be mowing the lawn – you'd be doing business with people, and with God. You'd be making a phone call to tell someone how much you appreciated them; you'd be writing a letter to put a wrong relationship right. You'd be focusing on your friends and family. That was the striking difference about the people I met in Peru. They didn't have the resources to buy lots of material goods, and they didn't live in a culture which focused on trivia. Instead, they spent their time with other people and they knew the value of friendship, fellowship and community, sharing the little they had.

Are you spending time on things that matter? Things that will have an impact on eternity? Or are you running round and round like a pet mouse on an exercise wheel, trapped by your possessions and your home and never really getting anywhere?

Stop and Think

Think back over the last few days. How many times did you put off something important – reading a bedtime story to a child, having a conversation with a friend, spending time with God – to deal with an interruption, answer the phone or tidy up because someone was coming? 'Your heavenly Father already knows all your needs and he will give you all you need from day to day if you live for him and make the Kingdom of God your primary concern' (Matthew 6:33).

The Living Room

4

Wanting What You Have

The living room is the one visitors are most likely to be invited into. What does it say about us and our lives?

Double-take

Television programmes and magazine articles are constantly encouraging us to look for ways of improving our lifestyle, to get a new look for spring or simply keep up with the latest fashions. Stand in the doorway of your living room and look slowly round the room. Imagine you're an interior designer on a home makeover programme. What would you change? Is the colour scheme out of date? Has the sofa seen better days? Do you need some 'storage solutions' to contain the magazines, the videos or your CD collection? If you replaced the sofa, carpets and curtains, how much would it cost? And how much difference would it actually make to your life? How soon would the fashion change so that your furnishings and colour schemes would be out of date once again?

Now look round the room again, but this time imagine you're a person from a developing country – Peru, or Kenya, or Burkina Faso. How does the room look now? In fact, it's full of unbelievable riches. How can anyone use all these things on a daily basis? How can anyone have sufficient money and leisure time to relax with all those books, CDs, magazines and videos? How could anyone want anything more?

It has been said that the secret of happiness is not having what you want; it's wanting what you already have. Studies of people who win the lottery suggest that even with the power to buy anything they could possibly want in life, they are no happier than anyone else once the initial excitement has worn off. Someone who appreciates everything they have as a gift from God – home, family, relationships, health, or just the joy of a sunny day – is much richer. They have the secret of tasting happiness every moment of the day.

Good stewardship

Now, it's true that most of the time we don't compare ourselves with someone living in a mud hut or a corrugated-iron shanty-town shack. We have to live in the place where we are and that means, to some extent, conforming to the norms of our society. We don't have to do without electricity just because many people don't have it. Neither should we feel guilty about what we have. But there are two very suitable responses to the 'double-take' exercise. First, count your blessings. Give thanks to God for what you have and take pleasure in your home. Don't take it for granted. Second, look at how you use what's there and use it wisely.

Stewardship isn't just about making sure we give to charity or support our church. It's about being responsible in the way we live. Our Western lifestyle makes disproportionate demands on our planet. We need to think seriously about our present levels of consumption and the way we use the world's natural resources. The world that our children and grandchildren will inherit is in danger – from climate change, pollution, exhausted resources and the social upheavals resulting from inequality between rich and poor. We have a wider responsibility to care for the planet God has given us as our home and for the people with whom we share it.

Electricity has been in use for 200 years, yet today 40 per cent of the world's population still have no access to it.

Surplus to requirements

How much is lurking on the shelves of your living room which is really surplus to requirements? Do you have videos of television programmes that you recorded but never got round to watching? CDs that you haven't listened to for ten years? (Or even vinyl records and audio cassettes, both beginning to seem like very old technology. Do you still have the equipment to play them, and do you ever use it?) Are there books on the bookshelf that you're never likely to want to read again?

There are two questions to ask. First, why do you keep all this stuff? Most likely you never get round to sorting it out until the clutter level becomes intolerable or you run out of space. But perhaps there are other reasons. Do you secretly hope that a good collection of books and CDs will make you look more of an intellectual than a couch potato? What does that say about your self-esteem and need to impress other people? Take it to the Lord in prayer and ask him to show you how precious you are in his sight.

Second, could some of those items be put to better use elsewhere? If you took them to the charity shop they could help other people twice: once when someone gets to buy a second-hand book more cheaply than a new copy, and again when the money goes to help Oxfam or Cancer Research or other charities. And you would benefit from the extra space!

I came, I saw, Ikea

If your home wouldn't pass the 'interior designer' test, if it's old and worn and nothing matches, how does that make you feel? Do you envy those who have more than you? Do you spend time planning improvements, looking through piles of glossy magazines, going round the shops looking for new furniture, or trying to get things colour co-ordinated? Do you have a pile of catalogues waiting for you to compare the merits of two almost identical shelving systems?

We have to ask ourselves what is important to us. Spending our days flicking through magazines in search of the most up-to-date 'look' is a waste of our time and attention, not least because as soon as we've invested in it the latest thing will have changed. That's how the designers and retailers make their living, after all.

Personally, I love visiting homes which have that 'lived in' look, because then I don't feel so bad about my own! When I go into homes where everything is pristine – with immaculate paintwork, perfect upholstery and carpets, and I have to take my shoes off when I go in – I feel uncomfortable. It makes me edgy and I'm sure to spill my coffee.

Confessions of a cushion-plumper

I used to be terribly fussy about keeping my home as perfect as I could. I liked everything to be tidy and clean, and it bothered me if things were out of place. At night I would always go round tidying up, plumping up the cushions and opening the curtains before I went to bed, so that the room would be nice to come down to in the morning.

Roy used to call me a 'cushion-plumper'. He said that I never enjoyed today properly, because I was always worrying about tomorrow. He was right. 'Don't worry about tomorrow, for tomorrow will bring its own worries' (Matthew 6:34). There's no point being concerned about what other people will think and trying to keep up standards in order to impress them. There's even less point in doing it for the sake of our families. There's a saying that goes, 'A home should be clean enough to be healthy, and messy enough to be happy.' Our children certainly won't thank us for keeping a perfect house if it means we're nagging them all the time to take off their shoes and following them round watching for spills and mess.

TV times

How much does television govern your time? Do you switch it on automatically when you come in and leave it talking to itself all evening? Do you find yourself flicking between channels, looking for something interesting? (Nowadays, with satellite and cable expanding the numbers of channels available to us, just channel-hopping could take up the whole evening.)

All of us have evenings when we're really too tired to do anything very much, and days when a good film gets us through an afternoon which would otherwise be made miserable by flu or a sick child. But it's so easy to stop making conscious decisions about whether to watch television. As soon as one programme finishes, we wait for the next to start in case it's interesting, and then our attention is caught by something we never planned to watch in the first place and won't remember tomorrow.

Of course, it's too much to hope that everything we watch will be memorable. But it's a good idea to look through the programme schedules and mark what we intend to watch. That way we at least have some idea of how many hours we've spent 'accidentally' watching television.

24 hours for free

The living room is probably the place where you spend most of your spare time, reading, watching television, or just being together with family or friends. How do you spend your time? Try filling in this time diary over the course of a week, and see what your priorities really are.

How many hours did you spend...	Mon	Tues	Wed	Thur	Fri	Sat	Sun	Total
Watching television								
Reading								
Cooking/eating								
Doing housework								
At work								
Travelling								
Gardening								
Enjoying leisure/ hobbies								
Doing church activities								
Spending time alone with God								
Doing voluntary work								

Some of the time allocated to these activities is decided for us. If we have a job and need to travel to it, for example, a large part of our day is already taken. But we still have weekends and evenings when we are free to choose how to spend our time. What does the diary reveal about our priorities?

Are we generous with our time? Think how much you appreciate people who give up their time to help you, whether it's teaching an evening class or giving you a lift in their car. There is an enormous need for help in voluntary organisations these days. Brownie and Cub packs have long waiting lists because they can't get enough adult helpers; charities need people to work in their shops; local groups advertise for volunteers to befriend lonely and disabled people. Even if you don't have much money, God gives you 24 hours for free every day. Could you share some of that time with others?

Taking Action

Saving energy: www.est.org.uk
Books: www.bookcrossing.com
Television: www.healthunit.org/physact/home/tv_off/
tvturn_off.htm
Volunteering: www.wearewhatwedo.org;
www.timebank.org.uk

Stop and Think

It's our thought life that determines our attitudes. 'Don't copy the behaviour and customs of this world, but let God change you into a new person by changing the way you think' (Romans 12:2). The NIV translates this verse as '. . .be transformed by the renewing of your mind'. We constantly need to work on our minds, to renew our attitude towards the way we live our lives, keeping us in line with God's will.

Which of the thoughts associated with the living room has spoken to you? What does God want you to do about it?

The Kitchen

5

Sharing with the World

Unless you live entirely on takeaway food or eat out, it's likely that you spend a fair amount of time in your kitchen. What's your kitchen like – and what's in your cupboards?

Playing the mandolin

How do you acquire gadgets in your kitchen? Are they impulse buys or gifts from friends? Perhaps you watched an aspirational cookery programme (or even one of those looped advertising videos they play in some hardware departments) and decided that you really needed a mandolin egg-slicer, an electric apple-corer or a machine for making julienne carrots.

I've got a food processor. It slices and chops and kneads and mixes and blends and probably does several other things I haven't discovered yet. It's a very labour-saving device when it comes to preparing food. That's just as well, because the last time I used it, it took me much longer to unpack it, find the right attachments, assemble them, take them apart, wash all the bits and put it away again (about 15 minutes) than it did to grate the four carrots I wanted (about two minutes). Consequently I hardly ever use it. It's one of the things that I really don't need, but it sits in a cupboard, taking up space and having to be cleaned.

The same goes for crockery and cutlery. It may be plain and functional or expensive and elegant, but do you really need all that you have? Could someone benefit from your surplus? We have a wonderful scheme in our church called the Sharing Project. If we hear of a particular need, such as someone who needs to be rehoused, perhaps because they are leaving a situation of domestic violence, we put out a request for help. Everyone in the church looks out all their excess 'stuff', from rugs and beds to plates and glasses, and we collect and deliver it. It's amazing how far you can get towards furnishing a flat just from things people were planning to dispose of, if only they could find a good home for them or get help with the transport.

Another local church holds a furniture sale every Saturday. They collect and deliver (it only takes a couple of strong helpers and a volunteer with a van), and all the proceeds go to charity.

Best before. . .

We can apply the same sort of critical eye to our food cupboards. Time flies when you're enjoying your food, and we often stockpile cans and packets in our larders without realising that they each bear a 'best before. . .' date. A regular check of those printed dates will often surprise us: surely it isn't a year since we bought that packet of dried herbs for the dish we never got round to making. Sometimes we try new recipes and purchase obscure ingredients for them, but maybe we only ever use a teaspoonful of them. Or perhaps we impulse-buy things at the supermarket, thinking that one day we'll have time to grind our own spices for an exotic curry.

We live with excess while other people starve. There is actually enough grain produced in the world to provide 3,000 calories per person per day (and that's without the fruit, vegetables and meat we produce). That's more than we need. We would all be overweight if we ate that much. The world as a whole is not starving. Yet because of the way the grain is used (feeding it to cattle to produce meat, for instance, or holding it in grain mountains so that governments can control the market price), it's not available to most people in the world.

Here in the West we throw away more food than most people in the developing world live on. We complain that there is so much choice available in our shops that it takes too long to walk round all the aisles in the supermarket. We see people standing in front of a shelf of 30 different kinds of yoghurt, talking on their mobile phone and saying, 'Is it the apricot yoghurt with the bits in that you like?' We are utterly spoiled for choice. When Julia first came back from Peru I remember her standing dumbstruck in a supermarket, completely overcome by the amount of food available there. She had become used to living in a culture where people ate to live, and didn't live to eat.

Fair trade for all

There's no point in feeling guilty about this on a personal level. It's the world we live in. (Though there are plenty of things we can do to make the world a better and fairer place for everyone – see the 'Taking Action' boxes in some chapters of this book.) But as Christians with a sense of responsibility we may want to look carefully at how we spend our money, and make sure that we are not being wasteful in our stewardship of the gifts God has given us.

Millions of farmers in the developing world depend on selling their crops to survive, but the odds are stacked against them. The rules of international trade are biased in favour of the rich nations and powerful companies. The Fairtrade Mark guarantees farmers in developing countries a fair and stable price for their products, which covers their costs and allows them to plan for the future. It includes a premium that is set aside for farmers and workers to spend on social and environmental improvements which benefit entire communities. Look at the Fairtrade website for the real-life stories of families and communities around the world whose lives have been transformed as a result. By buying Fairtrade foods – increasingly available in supermarkets as well as from church outlets – you enable people to help themselves, and promote social justice around the world.

'Give fair judgement to the poor and the orphan; uphold the rights of the oppressed and the destitute' (Psalm 82:3).

Seventy per cent of the world's population lives on only 30 per cent of the world's produce. For the cost of three cups of coffee from a station stall, you could feed and educate a child in Uganda for a week.

A load of rubbish

What goes into your bin? Did you know that over 25 million tonnes of household rubbish are collected each year in the UK? Most of this goes to landfill sites, but in fact around 60 per cent of it could be recycled.

There are three reasons why we should be concerned about this. First, there is increasing pressure on landfill sites in our small and crowded country. Second, the non-renewable resources of our planet are being depleted. Both of these factors have an effect on the environment. The third reason is that God has entrusted this planet to us as our home: 'The LORD God placed the man in the Garden of Eden to tend and care for it' (Genesis 2:15). We have a duty to treat our environment with respect, because it is God's creation, and to act responsibly in the way we live in it.

Of course, the statistics are so mind-boggling that it's hard to imagine that what one person does can make a difference, especially when you're standing by the sink with a baked-bean tin in your hand. Do you put it straight in the bin, or do you rinse it and carry it out to the recycling box? It's not a lot more effort, but will it make a difference?

In fact, local pressure groups – made up of individuals – have persuaded more and more councils to provide recycling points and kerbside collections. Our local council now manages to recycle around 60 per cent of waste, which is a significant development.

Each person in the UK produces around half a tonne of waste each year. Disposable nappies take 300 years to biodegrade.

What contribution can you make?

Reduce

- Use reusable shopping bags instead of supermarket carriers.
- Buy fresh produce loose, instead of packaged.
- Store food in resealable containers, not clingfilm or food bags.
- Invest in rechargeable batteries and long life light bulbs.
- Use one good multi-surface cleaner for all cleaning jobs to reduce the number of bottles under your sink!
- Save on energy by ensuring your home is properly insulated and hot water thermostats are not set unnecessarily high.
- Leaving television sets or hi-fi's on 'stand-by' uses almost as much electricity as having them switched on.

Reuse

- Keep carrier bags and reuse them.
- Use both sides of every piece of paper.
- Buy household products in refillable containers.
- Donate old magazines to waiting rooms.

Recycle

- Use your kerbside recycling box.
- Use recycling depots for things that can't be collected.
- Start a compost heap for kitchen and garden waste.
- Buy recycled products wherever possible.

Taking Action

Fairtrade: www.fairtrade.org.uk;
www.maketradefair.com; www.oxfam.org.uk
Waste: www.wasteonline.org.uk;
www.wastepoint.co.uk

Prayer

Father, please give me a wider vision of your world. Help me to respect your creation. Touch my heart with concern for those who suffer poverty and injustice, and give me the will to make changes in my comfortable life that will help other people. I ask it in Jesus' name. Amen.

The Dining Room

6

Food and Fellowship

In my house I don't have a separate dining room, just a dining area, and I keep my computer there, so it doubles as an office. Some people rarely use their dining rooms, except when they are entertaining: the rest of the time they eat their meals off their laps in front of the television. This isn't particularly good for the digestion, and it's even worse for conversation. Family mealtimes – even when everyone is leading a busy life and you struggle to get everyone together round the table at the same time – can be valuable for meeting together and talking over the events of the day.

We always used to have breakfast together as a family, when we would say a short prayer for the day ahead. We also had supper together as often as possible, which was harder than it sounds with four children all involved in different activities and hobbies and after-school clubs, and a husband who was often working away from home. At weekends, though, we would all manage to sit down regularly. On several occasions Roy hid a tape recorder under the table and made a recording of the organised mayhem that was a family meal:

'He's got more than me!'
'No, I haven't.'
'And then Miss Evans said. . .'
'Dad, can I go on the school trip?'
'You *have* got more than me.'
Thump. Wail.
'Mu-u-m, Ben hit me!'

Those tapes are a treasure for me now. They bring back all the fun and laughter and hard work of bringing up a family, as well as the day-to-day chatter of the children at different ages.

Bookshelf bonanza

How many cookery books do you own? People buy us lavishly illustrated books for Christmas and birthdays, and we spend time looking through them, but how much difference do they actually make to the quality of the food we cook on a daily basis? It's great if we use them to find ways of cooking well, and feeding ourselves and our families cheaply and nutritiously. But so often they imply a dinner-party lifestyle. How many times have you seen a magazine article entitled 'Cooking to Impress'? Have you ever reflected on the underlying assumptions? Should our aim only be to impress people? And should food ever be used for that purpose?

There's no need for us to cook only plain and boring food out of some misguided feeling that it's somehow morally superior. We should always do our very best and be as imaginative as we can with the resources we have, and cookery books can be a real help for that purpose. But it's a good idea to do a bookshelf reality check. Do I use it? Do I need it? Who am I trying to convince that I'm a fantastic cook – myself, my family, or my visitors?

It's easy to identify the books we really use. They're the ones that look a bit scruffy, that bear the occasional buttery fingerprint or splash of sauce. Look hard at any glossy cookery book that's still as good as new. Is it gathering dust? If so, take it to the charity shop.

The fear of failure

Why do we invite people for meals? Is it just to impress, to show off our culinary skills and our ability to choose good wine? Or is it from a genuine desire to enjoy people's company and to make them feel at home? The atmosphere and our motivation are far more important than our ability to cook a brilliant meal. Some of us are so lacking in confidence about the standard of our cooking or the acceptability of our homes that we don't even bother to make the effort and invite people. Yet the warmth of our welcome, the offer of our friendship and the experience of fellowship make a far greater impression on people than our *House Beautiful* standards.

My husband Roy used to love to tell the story of a Christmas party we gave, when I made the most enormous chocolate cheesecake. I followed the recipe exactly and put in all the exotic ingredients, the best chocolate and the double cream. It was inedible. No one could manage more than the first mouthful. He enjoyed telling people that by February even the birds hadn't managed to finish it! It was one of those total disasters – but it made us laugh. I was embarrassed at the time, but now I tell the story myself. Why do we worry about things being less than perfect? No one ever lost a real friend because the meal wasn't up to scratch.

A feast on the table

When Matthew the tax collector left everything to follow Jesus, Jesus didn't suggest that they hold a prayer meeting. Instead he invited himself to Matthew's house to meet his friends, who were described as notorious sinners. From the disapproval of the Pharisees, we often get the impression that Jesus was a man who knew how to enjoy himself. What can we learn from Jesus' willingness to be part of people's everyday lives in this way?

It's good to get together with family and friends to celebrate over a meal. Sharing food has always been a way of enjoying fellowship together, thanking God for his goodness and enjoying one another's company.

> This festival will be a happy time of rejoicing with your family . . . celebrate this festival to honour the LORD your God . . . for it is the Lord your God who gives you bountiful harvests and blesses all your work. This festival will be a time of great joy for all. (Deuteronomy 16:14–15)

We can learn to use our dining rooms as a means of fellowship, and not just with our fellow Christians. There is a real danger in spending so much time within the Christian community that we no longer have friends outside the church and begin to lose touch with the everyday culture of our society. How can we be yeast and salt if we never get mixed in?

If you want to reach your neighbours and friends, there are lots of ways you can use your home graciously to exercise your gift for hospitality and build the kind of relationships that open the way for easy communication – and eventually, perhaps, the opportunity to share the gospel. People rarely turn down a non-threatening invitation to a meal (provided they're sure they aren't letting themselves in for a Bible study). You can make opportunities to develop friendships in a relaxed atmosphere, with the potential for talking about your faith if the occasion arises. Generally it does.

One friend of mine hosted a champagne-tasting evening. It sounds ridiculously decadent and extravagant, but how else do you reach the people who are living a champagne lifestyle? You can only reach people where they are, so you have to go where the people are. Have a coffee morning, a charity evening, a Fairtrade chocolate-tasting or a 'Use your LOAF' (Local, Organic, Animal-friendly, Fairtrade) evening – whatever interests you or your neighbours. Reach out in love and genuine interest, and the opportunities for fellowship will multiply.

Also, I think we can decide to allow ourselves to lighten up a bit. It's easy to get so caught up with the seriousness of our calling to seek and save the lost that we forget to relax. We read books like this one, encouraging us to look hard at our lives and weed out anything which does not glorify God, and before we know it we are toiling through life with furrowed brows, desperately earnest in our desire for holiness. We are not wrong to want to do the best we can, but we mustn't become too guilt-ridden or too holier-than-thou.

Let's stop working in the kitchen like Martha for a minute, and sit at the feet of the Master, like Mary.

Even so, I have noticed one thing, at least, that is good. It is good for people to eat well, drink a good glass of wine, and enjoy their work – whatever they do under the sun – for however long God lets them live . . . To enjoy your work and accept your lot in life – that is indeed a gift from God. People who do this rarely look with sorrow on the past, for God has given them reason for joy. (Ecclesiastes 5:18–20)

Taking Action

Outreach: www.faithworks.info; www.activatecv.org.uk

Stop and Think

I visited a church in Hurstpierpoint, West Sussex, one Sunday morning and found that they weren't in the church building at all. Once a month they close the church and instead open up the village hall, where they make brunch and serve coffee and croissants. They run a children's fun area, have a place where adults can sit and chat, and have all the Sunday papers available. Halfway through the morning they interview someone (me, on that occasion) and have someone to review the newspapers. It's a focus for dozens of people who would never dream of going to a church service, and it centres, unthreateningly, around the sharing of food.

The Study

7

Time and Money

The study is a great place for accumulating clutter – old papers, notes from meetings and articles cut from magazines which you know, deep down, you'll never refer to again. If this is the place where you put all the post as it arrives, or where you keep the bills until they're due to be paid, you may find yourself with piles of important and fairly recent papers which nevertheless make it difficult for you to find anything, or to remember when the due date comes around. What can you do to make life easier for yourself?

Paper chase

If you find yourself conducting a sort of archaeological dig for documents, then it's time to impose some order on your paperwork. Make up your mind that you'll get organised, and be prepared to be ruthless. Buy a set of cheap cardboard folders, some sticky labels and a big fat marker pen. (It's amazing how much better the situation seems once everything is labelled.) Then allocate an afternoon to sorting.

Separate older items from current papers and bills await-
ing payment, then work out what actually needs to be kept.
For instance, if you are self-employed, there are special
rules about what you need for tax purposes. Check how
long you need to keep those receipts and invoices, as it may
be possible to throw many of them away. Make up folders,
label them with the contents and the date by which they
can be discarded, and file everything neatly. If you really
must keep items of interest, magazine articles, etc., make
them a folder of their own.

After that, try to handle paper only once: open it, make a
decision (or write the cheque, etc.) and file it. Don't put it
in a pile.

There's no doubt that it takes a certain amount of time to
do the administrative work around running a household,
and we're fooling ourselves if we think it gets done in some
sort of 'magic' time which we'll find somewhere. That's
why things get left to gather dust. Allocate some time for
these chores and do them regularly. If you are really finding
it hard to make the time, watch out for a deeper problem
that afflicts so many of us – excessive busyness.

Addicted to urgency

Some people are always in a rush; they give the impression
of having far too much to do and being constantly in
demand from all sides. Is this you? Do you believe that the
reason you don't find time to clear your clutter is that you
are far too busy to get round to such mundane jobs?

It's possible to be addicted to a sense of urgency. Always
being busy allows us to feel needed, gives us a sense of

getting things done and falsely enhances our self-esteem. On the other hand, it also eats time, stops us estimating the true value of various competing activities and often causes us to hurry and make mistakes. Most of all, it robs us of the ability to relax and fully enjoy our leisure time.

Busyness gives an impression of status, and may make others unwilling to trespass on our 'valuable' time. How painful would it be to discover that we could have helped someone, but they were too timid to ask for a share of our time?

This is another thing to take to God in prayer. We need the humility of Jesus, who had time for everyone, however humble. When he was on his way to heal Jairus's daughter – an urgent errand if ever there was one – a sick woman in the crowd touched the fringe of his robe. At once he stopped and spoke to her: 'Who touched my clothes?' The disciples thought it was ridiculous for him to think that he had identified one touch among a jostling crowd, but he was sensitive to her need. When the woman told him what she had done, he said, 'Daughter, your faith has made you well. Go in peace. You have been healed' (Mark 5:24–34). We need to be able to identify the tasks that God wants us to do and organise our time so that we can address them.

If you think that you are suffering from busyness, have the courage to make some changes to your lifestyle. It will be beneficial not only for you, but also for your loved ones and your relationship with them. If you are always under pressure to give up your time to good causes or church activities, learn to say no without guilt, so that when you do say yes, you can say it without reserve or fear that you won't be able to fit it in. If you encounter misunderstanding

('Why? You're not ill, are you?'), don't worry. You know why you're cutting back on activity.

Once, when I had taken on far too much, someone rang me with a request for a speaking engagement. I supported the charity involved and I hated to turn them down, though I couldn't begin to think how I would find the time to prepare a talk, let alone the energy to give it. The best I could manage on the phone was to put them off for an hour or so. I said I would ring back when I had looked in my diary and tried to rearrange a few things, but it wasn't possible.

Roy saved me from too much despondency. 'If you say no, it won't be a big deal,' he said. 'It only means that the organiser will have to make a few more phone calls, and search around until he finds someone who says yes. That's his problem, not yours, and who knows? You might be helping someone else discover a new gift for speaking, if they're invited to give the talk. No one's indispensable.'

The dee dah day

There's a wonderful passage in *The Sacred Diary of Adrian Plass* where Adrian, as a study group leader, decides that he must be totally available to help the members of his group with any problem – from theological doubts to fixing tap washers – and as a result is out every night, neglecting his own home and marriage. In the end he responds to a note saying that an abandoned family has turned up in a local café and rushes there to help, only to find his wife and son waiting for him. A sense of proportion is always important!

How well do you juggle the various pressures on your time? Have you managed to achieve a balance between work, leisure activities and church, or does your family lose out in the competition for your attention? What could you sacrifice to make sure that you spend more time with your wife, your husband or your children?

In John Ortberg's book, *The Life You've Always Wanted*, he describes bathing his three children. One child was still in the tub, one was safely in her pyjamas, and he was trying to get Mallory dried. She, however, was doing what was known in his family as 'the dee dah day dance' – running around in circles singing 'Dee dah day, dee dah day' over and over again. It was her way of expressing great joy, when her six-year-old exuberance became too great to contain.

'Hurry up, Mallory,' her father said in irritation, so she did: she ran round faster. 'That's not what I meant,' he said. 'Get over here, quickly.'

Then Mallory asked a profound question: 'Why?'

It stopped her father in his tracks. He had nothing else waiting to be done, and it was his children's bedtime. He was just so used to hurrying that he couldn't see when to stop. 'Here was life; here was joy; here was an invitation to the dance, right in front of me, and I was missing it.'

So he got up and joined Mallory in the dee dah day dance. 'She said I was pretty good at it, too, for a man of my age.'

The way John Ortberg describes his thought processes is probably true of many of us. He says he tended to divide his time between 'living' and 'waiting to live'. Time spent hurrying from one place to another, or from one task to another, is time when he is unlikely to be fully present, or aware of the voice and purpose of God.

It's easy, especially when we're tired after a busy day, to

just try to 'get through' our various tasks so that we can relax. Yet the meaning of our lives is made up of these trifling interactions with our loved ones, and with God, and they can make all the difference to our happiness and the quality of our relationships.

It has often been said that you'll never find a man on his deathbed saying, 'I wish I'd spent more time at the office!' When eulogies are given at funerals, people rarely talk about the deceased in terms of how much money, property or stocks and shares they accumulated. Instead, they focus on their relationships with others. What will your legacy be? Will it be like the fragrance of perfume that lingers after the person has left the room? Will you be passing on the values of a loving partner, a wise parent or a mentor to others – work that takes a lifetime of daily investment in time and care?

Surfing or drifting?

Do you have a computer in your study? It can be a wonderful aid to efficiency – printing all our Christmas card address labels in a fraction of the time it would take to write them, enabling us to keep track of our finances with spreadsheets, and keeping us in touch with distant friends by email. But it can also be a tremendous thief of time, drawing us into hours of internet surfing, the electronic equivalent of flicking through a magazine.

Try keeping a record of how much time you spend in a week surfing the internet, shopping online, visiting chat rooms or playing computer games (you might like to add to that any time you spend on a Playstation if you have one).

It can be a surprise to see where the time goes. Could you be doing something more useful?

There are also insidious temptations lurking in the grey box on the desk, more serious than the mere time-wasting activity of surfing the net. Many honest Christian men and women have risked a look at pornographic material and have found themselves spending more and more time doing so. Often they haven't even gone looking for it initially; we all know how often random emails arrive with unpleasant, distasteful and disturbing content, linking you straight to a site you would never have visited otherwise. The initial attraction may be curiosity – either to see what all the fuss is about, or seeking more knowledge about sexual activity. Some people are able to turn away, but many more drift into addiction to the illicit excitement and apparent intimacy of viewing sex on the internet. 'You are a slave to whatever controls you' (2 Peter 2:19).

The tragedy is that pornography often has the effect of making real relationships more difficult, because of guilt or secrecy. Elaine Storkey wrote in her book *The Search for Intimacy*, 'The saddest thing is that pornography can never be a substitute for relating to another human being. It can only widen the loneliness.'

Research indicates that 33 per cent of all UK internet users view pornography online, and Christians are not excepted: Christian Viewpoint for Men estimates that one in five Christian men have an 'Achilles heel' for pornography. The Christian organisation CARE received so many calls from British Christians asking for help that they recently published a list of online resources to help break the bonds of this addiction. There are several organisations now willing to offer help, supporting people with prayer and fellowship. One recommended method is to join an accountability group, where people seek to support and be accountable to each other. The internet system called Covenant Eyes uses this principle: when you subscribe, it logs every website accessed from your computer and sends a report (scoring all entries for pornography) to two accountability partners. Once the protection of anonymity and secrecy is gone, people find it much easier to resist the temptation.

Lance de Vries, Operations Director of Christian Viewpoint for Men, says, 'If porn is a problem for you then ask the Lord to forgive you – for the thousandth time, if necessary, for he is faithful to do it (1 John 1:9) – and commit to him to repent and change. Find that trusted person and confess the sin, shining the light of truth on it and robbing it of its power. Then get all the help you need, including internet accountability.'

Money, money, money

The study is also the place for examining our finances, and that computer spreadsheet (if you're clever enough to build one) may be telling you something you'd rather ignore. Personal debt is an increasing problem in our society. The Citizens' Advice Bureau estimates that around six million families in the UK are struggling to keep up with their credit commitments. It's easy to obtain loans and even easier to run up huge bills on credit cards, and the fact that this is so common can blunt our conscience about the way we use our money.

The Citizens' Advice Bureau sees around one million people with debt problems each year. Consumer debt (credit and store cards and loans) accounts for two thirds of these.

Have you allowed yourself to get into debt because you wanted the same kind of holidays as your neighbours? Have you spent more than you should to keep up with friends? Maybe you can't understand how everyone else seems to manage when you can't, or perhaps your children have blackmailed you into buying the latest designer trainers or clothes. Have you been so carried away by advertising or the annual spending frenzy that you've spent too much at Christmas and find yourself paying for it for the rest of the year? Is worry about money consuming your peace of mind?

There is an excellent book by Rob Parsons called *The Money Secret* (Hodder and Stoughton, 2005). It tackles the issues of debt and financial pressure, exposes many of the scams operated by lenders, and shows us how to address our problems and make wise decisions in the future.

This is another area where the spiritual side of decluttering comes into its own. It enables us to see just how far we have been seduced by the world's standards and priorities. When we're spending time tidying away those bank and credit card statements, it pays to think and pray about how we spend our money, and ask ourselves whether we can justify how we use it. 'Beware! Don't be greedy for what you don't have. Real life is not measured by how much we own' (Luke 12:15).

If we are addicted to shopping, we have to ask ourselves

why. Do we always feel needy, so that buying something new briefly gives us a buzz of satisfaction which is soon over, leaving us dissatisfied once again? If we are constantly buying things to fill a void in our lives, we need to look again at what we need. The Bible promises that God will supply all our needs. If you are overspending on a regular basis, take your problem to the Lord in prayer, and ask him to show you how his grace can satisfy the deepest needs of your heart.

Taking Action

Computers: www.computer-aid.org; www.tfs.org.uk
Help for pornography addiction: www.care.org.uk; www.cvmen.org.uk; www.covenanteyes.com
Money: www.citizensadvice.org.uk; www.themoneysecret.info

Prayer

Lord Jesus, you came so that we might have life, and have it more abundantly. Help me to see the poverty of my spirit, and open my heart so that you can fill it with your love. Amen.

The Bedroom

8

Meeting Your Real Needs

Physical clutter in the bedroom can interfere with the relaxed atmosphere you want to create, so go ahead and tidy up, being ruthless with odd socks, discarded tissues and dirty washing. At the same time, look more carefully at your bedroom and see if it sheds light on your underlying assumptions and expectations. What can it tell you about the way you live your life?

What's in the wardrobe?

Is your wardrobe so full that it's hard to get anything more in? Are your clothes so cramped for space that they need ironing when they're taken out? What is on your 'to buy' list at the moment?

Clothes shopping is connected to our feelings about our appearance: we need to be clean and tidy, and some jobs require a certain level of smart dressing. Somehow we take these basics and extend them until we find it hard to distinguish 'needing' from 'wanting'. With encouragement from shops and magazines, we could go on buying clothes for ever, spending ridiculous amounts of money. Even the articles promising 'catwalk fashion at high-street prices' are not designed to save you money, in spite of the clever wording. They are designed to encourage you to spend more. If you wouldn't have considered the latest fashion when the price tag was £1,000, why is it suddenly more necessary to your lifestyle when it's £200?

A young man I know told me about a dreadful shopping expedition with his girlfriend. They spent hours touring the shops, looking at designer boots. At last he spotted a pair which seemed ideal, but she dismissed them at once: 'They're *so* last year!'

Some people seem to get addicted to buying shoes or handbags. Why do we do it? We all understand about 'comfort eating' – when stress or distress makes you feel constantly hungry, so that the chocolate bar or cream cake is suddenly irresistible (funny how a carrot or a stick of celery doesn't do the trick). For some people, the same kind of stress, loneliness or unhappiness produces a similar feeling of emptiness, which can only be assuaged by 'comfort buying'. It fills the wardrobe, but it empties the bank account. Even high-street accessories can add up to a sizeable investment if you choose to cheer yourself up by buying a new pair of earrings or bangles every time you feel down.

If your wardrobe is bulging, try making an inventory. What has not been worn for two years? What are you waiting to slim into – and unless you're currently pregnant, do you really believe you will? Clear it out and take it to the charity shop, and resist the temptation to restock. In fact, try 'fasting' from clothes buying for a year. Nothing will look hopelessly out of date if you're wearing it for just one more season, and just think of all the time you'll save by not browsing around the shops. There isn't any point if you know you're not going to buy anything.

If that feels like a tremendous deprivation to you, and shopping is one of your major leisure activities, go back to the time chart you filled out. How important is shopping in relation to the other ways you spend your time? 'Wherever your treasure is, there your heart and thoughts will also be' (Matthew 6:21). Has it assumed a disproportionate import-ance in your life?

If you are an impulse-buyer, ask yourself why. Perhaps you feel that you deserve new things as a treat to make up for other parts of your life which are not particularly rewarding, or to reassure yourself that you are worth spending money on. Whatever you think the cause may be, take it to the Lord in prayer and ask him to show you what is lacking. In his eyes you are always worth his time, attention and love. He loved you so much that he sent his Son to die for you. How can buying trinkets compare with that?

> *'Retail therapy is the equivalent of a throat lozenge when what we need is ointment for the soul.'*
>
> *Rob Parsons*

The baggage in the bedroom

The baggage in the bedroom isn't just clothes. There's a verse in the Bible that says, 'Do not let the sun go down on your anger' (Ephesians 4:26 NRSV), but how many of us take it into the bedroom with us? There's the baggage of past relationships and bad relationships, and of arguments and recriminations that can sour our happiness.

If you have a partner, you may find it easy to punish him or her with silence and isolation at bedtime. Yet the bedroom can be the place where reconciliation happens and where problems are shared and solved. 'Love does not demand its own way. It is not irritable, and it keeps no record of when it has been wronged' (1 Corinthians 13:5). However hard we find it to keep to the first part of this (which of us is never irritable?), we should always keep to the second part and refuse to brood over wrongs. Better to bring our resentments out into the open, calmly and lovingly, and talk them through if we can. Often we find that the perceived 'wrong' was accidental and unintended and can be swiftly forgiven.

You may live alone but still be holding on to the anger and bitterness of a broken relationship or divorce. These are hard to let go of, and keeping no record of wrongs can be a challenge indeed in these circumstances. Yet we are injuring ourselves by reliving those pains and preventing ourselves from moving on. Take your troubles to the Lord, and ask for his help. Some people find a Bible verse that relates well to the situation they are grieving over and memorise it. Then, every time they find themselves back on that old treadmill of thought, going over what was said (or what they wish they had said), they catch themselves, stop and recite their verse. Soon they are able to prevent the replaying of that mental video of painful scenes and look forward with new hope.

The two o'clock club

If I'm awake at two a.m. and feeling lonely in the darkness, I often think about all the other people who are awake at the same time: the mothers with new babies, the carers watching by sickbeds, the nurses and police and other night workers. It's a busy night-time world out there! Yet the real members of the two o'clock club are not those who are working but the people who simply can't sleep.

A lot of thinking goes on in the small hours, when things keep going round and round in our heads. Many of our fears remain unspoken during the day, but anxiety increases in the dark of the night. What is causing that pain? Could it be cancer? What is really troubling that teenager? Problems about work, home, children, health, money, the future; embarrassment about things we've said or wrong decisions we've made; hurtful comments that other people have made to us. We lie awake in the night thinking them through and unable to escape from the prison of our own minds.

Grief is often confined to the bedroom. When my husband died I made a deliberate decision to be as 'normal' as I could with my friends. I recognised that many people lose their friends when they are constantly moaning and negative, and I didn't want to be one of those. But in the security of my bedroom I shed many tears before my heavenly Father who understood my pain, my loneliness and my loss.

There's only one place to put all these things, and that's at the foot of the cross. Nothing is beyond the reach of God's love and the power of the Holy Spirit to calm our fears, forgive our sins and heal those deep wounds.

A purpose for pain

When we are weary and worried, it's hard to believe that any good can come out of our troubles. Yet we know that God can bring blessings out of any situation. The experiences which have caused us the most pain – through grief, hurt, or loss of expectation – can provide the potential for our greatest ministry. Who is better qualified to help the parents of a child who has died than the parents who have already walked that path? Who can reach out in true sympathy to the deserted wife, but one who truly understands her situation?

> All praise to the God and Father of our Lord Jesus Christ. He is the source of every mercy and the God who comforts us. He comforts us in all our troubles so that we can comfort others. When others are troubled, we will be able to give them the same comfort God has given us. (2 Corinthians 1:3–4)

We can use our own struggles and pain to glorify God by helping others who are in trouble.

Stop and Think

- Try making a list of all the things you are anxious about, and pray through each one of them. Then destroy your list in some way that makes sense to you: burn it, shred it or drop it in the river and watch it float away.

- Write out a favourite Bible verse of comfort and keep it by your bedside for reference in the small hours.
- Is there a word of comfort or encouragement that you could give to anyone you know?

The Bathroom

9

What Are Your Worries?

What colour is your bathroom suite? If it's the dreaded avocado, don't worry. In 20 years' time, your children will be delighted that you have the most fashionable suite in town, and everyone else will be throwing out the plain white ones. Why do we bother at all about fashions, as long as it works?

In the shanty town where my daughter Julia lived, many homes didn't even have running water. Julia felt incredibly privileged to have a cold tap in her house. Her neighbours' poverty makes choosing colours and styles of sanitary ware seem rather frivolous.

In the UK we take our bathrooms for granted. Good sanitation and clean water are part of our lives that we scarcely ever think about – we even use water that has been cleaned to drinking quality standard to flush our toilets. The briefest water shortages and resulting hosepipe bans fill us with surprise and indignation. Yet millions of people all over the world never have access to water as clean as the stuff we pour onto our geraniums.

2.4 billion people in the world do not have access to adequate sanitation and 20 per cent of the world's population does not have safe water to drink.

Saving water in this country won't help the children dying of water-related diseases in Africa – unless, of course, we think more carefully about our money. It's amazing how a water meter changed my attitude to water consumption. It made me realise how negligent I was about leaving taps running and using a hose to wash the car. If you're using a water meter, check out your consumption and take some steps to reduce it.

- Don't let the tap run while you're cleaning your teeth.
- Shower more often than you bath.
- Use washing-up water on the garden.

Look for the difference in your water bills, and give the money you save to help someone else have clean water. And if we all do it, maybe we won't have a hosepipe ban next year.

Skin deep

What we see when we look in the bathroom mirror concerns us all. Magazine articles encourage us to examine our skin for blemishes or wrinkles and offer us hundreds of preparations to deal with everything – dry skin, oily skin, combination skin; cleansers, toners, moisturisers, blushers, concealers, mascara, lipstick. How much old or unused make-up do you have lurking in the bathroom cupboard?

Part of the trouble is the unreal cult of celebrity, which presents us with pictures of impossible beauty in magazines and films. We forget that the carefree-looking film star or the smiling cover girl has just spent an arduous three hours with a make-up artist, and that any imperfections in the photographs have been airbrushed out. If we saw those same women without make-up, standing in the queue in the supermarket, we probably wouldn't give them a second look. Yet 99 per cent of us look at the 1 per cent who are supermodels and celebrities and feel that we fall short.

We all know how ephemeral physical beauty is: everyone ages, and time changes our appearance. The most dissatisfied women, and those who find it hardest to come to terms with the changes in face and body that middle age can bring, are often those who had a high opinion of their looks in youth and became dependent on the admiring looks of others. Yet a middle-aged face which has character can be far more attractive than one which has been endlessly lifted and botoxed into a mask. Think of some of our best-loved actresses – Helen Mirren, Judi Dench, Maggie Smith, Julie Walters: none of them is attempting to look like a woman half her age, yet they bring warmth and experience to every role they play.

Most of what we describe as beauty is actually just a set of symmetrical features. People seem to be programmed to prefer symmetry in a face, possibly because it may be an indicator of good health. Yet we know that we don't choose our friends by their looks and that appearance is no indicator of character, honesty, reliability, unselfishness or the ability to love. The people who really love us don't do so because of our appearance. God doesn't care about pretty people more than plain ones, so why do we worry so much about how we look?

True beauty

What is true beauty in the eyes of God? If we look at the first letter of Peter, we can pick out three significant elements.

- *Purity*. 'Your godly lives will speak to them better than any words. They will be won over by your pure, godly behaviour' (1 Peter 3:1–2). This doesn't mean that God expects sinless perfection from us. He knows that we are human, fallible people. But if we have consecrated our lives to him, we will always be striving to be the best we can, choosing self-control over self-indulgence, costly honesty over easy evasion, and spiritual single-mindedness over the double standards of the world.

- *Modesty*. 'Don't be concerned about the outward beauty that depends on fancy hairstyles, expensive jewels or beautiful clothes' (1 Peter 3:3). Knowing that Jesus died for us gives us the greatest possible confidence in our self-worth. We know we are precious to him, and that means that he loves us as we are and for all that we can become. We don't need to draw attention to our bodies through extravagant or revealing fashions.

- *Serenity*. 'You should be known for the beauty that comes from within, the unfading beauty of a gentle and quiet spirit, which is so precious to God' (1 Peter 3:4). We can only have a gentle and quiet spirit if we are trusting in God's fatherly love. That confidence enables us to weather all the storms of life, turning to him with every need, every anxiety and every sorrow.

Tony Sargent, Principal of the International Christian College in Glasgow, described an aspect of true beauty in a recent prayer letter. He was preaching at a conference in Africa when an abandoned baby was placed in his arms.

And I meet one of the wealthiest women I have ever had the privilege to encounter. She pulls out a small portfolio and I go through it. Page after page, child after child. She rescued the lot – gave care until she was able to place them and writes a digest of them all. Somewhere in *Les Miserables* Hugo gets one of his characters to say that in looking into the face of human kindness you look into the face of God. I know what he means. I saw it and it leaves an abiding impression. Not a slim lady who would turn the heads of men – well endowed, wholesome. Eschewing fashion, this American saint exudes a beauty of which the Bible speaks so clearly, the inner beauty of a person right with God and untouched by secular values. Blessed sermon, a living epistle . . . more eloquent than any of mine.

Worried well

Maybe it's not your looks that concern you, but your health. What do you have in your bathroom cabinet? Is yours a sticking plaster and paracetamol household, or do you have lots of pills and potions? Does a cupboard full of cold cures, over-the-counter medicines or alternative remedies make you feel safer and better able to face the future?

Worries about our health can be all-consuming. It's easy to allow ourselves to be fearful about losing our health in

the future, especially as we get older. Yet our heavenly
Father will care about us just as much in the future as he
does today. Our anxiety can be a sign of our lack of trust
in God.

This always reminds me about the man at the pool of
Bethesda, who had been an invalid for many years. People
believed that if a disabled person went into the water when
it was stirred, he would be healed. The man had never managed it, because he had no one to help him and someone
else always got there first. Jesus saw the man lying there
and asked him an incredibly important question: 'Do you
want to get well?' (John 5:1–9).

*In developing countries, 30,000 people a day die because
medicines are too expensive.*

It might seem to have an obvious answer – who would not
want to be healed? And yet we know that it's not at all as
simple as it might appear. Many of us live behind the excuse
of not being well, and thus fail to enjoy what God wants to
give us and fulfil what he wants us to do. Having an illness,
a disability or just a minor ailment can be a safe place to be.
No one can ask us to do more, to exert all our energies or
try something new and challenging if we aren't very well.
In first-century Israel a man who had been disabled for so
long probably had no means of earning a living except beg-
ging. Jesus was challenging him to face life in a completely
new way. The man rose to the challenge: at a word from
Jesus, he picked up his mat and walked.

Long ago, before I became a Christian, I suffered from
depression. I felt guilty about it because on the face of things

I had everything I could ever want: a loving husband, a beautiful home, four happy, healthy children and enough money. Yet my life had changed so much. From enjoying a career in show business, I now faced the day-to-day struggles of family life with small children and a husband who was often away from home. I often felt tired, lonely and a failure.

It was only after a friend had shown me that in spite of my years of church-going I had never really encountered the living Saviour, and helped me to open my heart to Jesus, that I was released from my depression. My illness had been born out of self-pity and had become a way of gaining attention for me and my problems. Once I had made Jesus the Lord of my life, I discovered a new way of living. I realised that even if I was never noticed in my life again, I would still be running, leaping and dancing for joy. God cared for me! I had a new purpose, and even though I still faced all the same irritations and challenges of everyday life, I had renewed strength to face my tasks.

Not every depression is like this, and for many people the best and proper way to tackle it is with medication, but we should always accompany our medical treatment with prayerful trust in God, so that we can face the challenge of being well again.

Sometimes it's less easy to find the cause of our anxiety. In this context we also have to ask ourselves whether we are allowing ourselves to continue to be victims of our past. Perhaps we blame our difficulties on our upbringing, or some abusive relationship which has made it hard for us to trust. We know that Paul himself had problems ('a thorn in my flesh', 2 Corinthians 12:7–8), but he refused to allow the hurts of the past to affect his future, or to keep him from finishing his task. 'I press on. . .' (Philippians 3:12).

We mustn't let our past rob us of our future. Yesterday ended at midnight; tomorrow is another day. Let's lay the past to rest and move on, in hope and expectation of our Father's goodness and in the joy and peace that Jesus promises us. 'I am leaving you with a gift – peace of mind and heart. And the peace I give isn't like the peace the world gives. So don't be troubled or afraid' (John 14:27).

Taking Action

Water: www.wateraid.org.uk; www.h2ouse.org; www.environment-agency.gov.uk/subjects/waterres

Prayer

Lord Jesus, be with us when we are anxious or ill. Help us to lay aside our fears for the future, our anxieties about our appearance, and all the trivial concerns which fill our minds and prevent us from experiencing the peace of living in your love. Teach us to rest in you, and to walk with you every day of our lives, in courage and joy. Amen.

The Spare Room

10

Making Space for Others

Is your spare room a dumping ground for the clutter which has spilled over from the rest of the house? Is there room for visitors' clothes and belongings, or have you taken up space there with the surplus from other rooms? In fact, is there room in your life for visitors?

Angels or fish?

The Bible says, 'Don't forget to show hospitality to strangers, for some who have done this have entertained angels without knowing it' (Hebrews 13:2). Sometimes it doesn't quite feel like that – we may resent the intrusion into our routine, the extra work and cooking, and the necessity of sharing our time and attention with others.

Having other people in the house can be hard work, but do we make them feel welcome or uncomfortable? My mother used to laugh about a saying: 'Visitors are like fish – after three days they start to go off a bit.' In fact she always had the house full of visitors, and she was a wonderful and welcoming hostess, but I sometimes recognise the feeling.

After a few days we want to get on with our own lives. Our unselfishness doesn't have much staying power.

We have to be willing to recognise other people's needs and to sacrifice time which we'd rather spend on ourselves by giving it to other people. Perhaps you know someone who would like to break a long journey by staying with you overnight; perhaps you know students who don't have a place to stay, or foreign students who would love to spend time with a family at weekends, when they may be missing their homes. These are all opportunities not just to serve others, but to live out the gospel and demonstrate the love of Jesus to all sorts of people.

Brave new world

There's no point in harking back to a so-called Golden Age, but it is true that in the past communities were smaller and more connected. Our modern world is much more socially fragmented.

- People are much more mobile, and often live far away from their families.
- With televisions and computers in so many homes, people find their entertainment indoors and are less likely to take part in other activities.
- Long working hours mean that fewer people have the time or energy to engage in voluntary work.

All this means that there is more social isolation, which can have devastating effects on people's quality of life. Indifference presents a profound threat to our society, from neglected children and desperate and isolated parents, to the elderly who often live alone.

As Christians we may scarcely notice this: church fellowships provide strong bonds and support networks for all their members. If we don't have many contacts in the world outside our church, we may not realise what a profound lack of social contacts there may be in our neighbourhoods. Yet it is an urgent and increasing need, which social services and voluntary agencies struggle to meet and churches are ideally placed to help. It was this situation that prompted Steve Chalke to start the organisation Faithworks, which exists 'to empower and inspire individual Christians and every local church to develop their role at the hub of their community'. Faithworks provides resources, ideas and training to enable churches to fill some of the gaps in the social service network, and operates at a professional level to help some of the neediest people in our communities.

In our church we have a scheme called Befrienders, which links volunteers with people who are in need of help or friendship. The trained volunteers meet and befriend the individuals they are assigned to and support them over a long or short period. Sometimes people are referred to us by the doctor, social worker or health visitor; others come from contacts made by our community worker. It's a way in which the church can offer a Christian response to people in need.

Around 14 per cent of older people report that they never chat to neighbours. Around 21 per cent of older people do not see a friend or relative at least once a week. Around 12 million people in the UK are taking anti-depressants.

Doing good

Making space in our lives for other people is fundamental to our Christian faith. But it's important to remember that we don't do 'good deeds' in order to earn favour with God (or anyone else). Our salvation has been assured by the sacrifice of Christ on the cross. Rather, it is the life of Christ within us that is expressed in our actions and in our desire to reach out to others in love. 'Your generosity to them will prove that you are obedient to the Good News of Christ. And they will pray for you with deep affection because of the wonderful grace of God shown through you' (2 Corinthians 9:13–14).

If we are wondering what exactly we should be doing, we are like the man who asked Jesus, 'Who is my neighbour?' The Good Samaritan reacted in a positive and practical way to a need which he came across in the street. He didn't plan it, he had no agenda and he didn't pass by because he had an urgent committee meeting. If we keep our eyes open we will see the people God has placed in our path who need something that we can give – our love, our care, our time or our support. 'He has created us anew in Christ Jesus, so that we can do the good things he planned for us long ago' (Ephesians 2:10).

Your spare room doesn't have to be filled with needy people all the time, but it can act as a reminder to make space in your life for others. What seems like a poor use of time in your busy day – having coffee with a friend – may be the opportunity they need to talk about a problem. You don't have to have any solutions; just listening helps. Or volunteer for some activity which will reach people who are lonely and isolated. Remember Jesus' words, 'When you did it to one of the least of these my brothers and sisters, you were doing it to me' (Matthew 25:40).

Taking Action

Housing: www.shelter.org.uk
Volunteering: www.contact-the-elderly.org;
www.wrvs.org.uk; www.faithworks.info

Stop and Think

Christ has no body now on earth but yours,
no hands but yours,
no feet but yours.
Yours are the eyes through which he looks compassion on the world.
Yours are the feet with which he is to go about doing good.
Yours are the hands with which he is to bless men now.

St Thérèse of Lisieux

The Children's Rooms

11

Growing Healthy Relationships

Are your children's rooms calm and tidy – fun places to play and restful places to sleep? No, I thought not. Mine very seldom were, either!

Clutter-free kids

We may be happy about working towards a simpler lifestyle for ourselves, but if we have children, how far are we justified in imposing this on them? We don't want them to become angry and rebellious because they feel that we are depriving them of things, or worse still that an over-zealous parent has just taken half their toys to the charity shop. 'Do not make your children angry by the way you treat them. Rather, bring them up with the discipline and instruction approved by the Lord' (Ephesians 6:4).

What does this mean? Clearly, we are not supposed to indulge our children's every whim. That would be poor discipline. We have all read about parents who allow themselves to be bullied into buying expensive toys and designer clothes, ruining themselves financially and preventing their children from understanding the word 'no'. Although they are readily swayed by advertising and by what their friends have, children are capable at a remarkably early age of understanding a reasoned argument – even if it amounts to nothing more than 'We can't afford it'. A child who never hears these words will probably find it difficult to control his or her own spending in later life.

If you want to reduce the piles of toys, make sure that you and other relatives are a little more modest in your gift-buying. Being too ruthless with the massive amounts of 'stuff' that already infest our children's rooms will probably annoy them. They need to be allowed to make the decisions about their own belongings. Depending on their ages, we can begin to explain and develop their awareness of the needs of other people. It is very heartening at times of disaster (like the Asian tsunami of 2004) to see how children empathise with people who are suffering, and are eager to donate their pocket money or their time to fundraising. Years of *Blue Peter* appeals have proved this!

Toddler chic

Among the toys and books in your children's bedrooms, are there also bags of outgrown clothes? After bringing up four children myself, I would always say, 'Never keep any clothes for best.' They'll be outgrown before they're outworn. At our church we have a group called 'Pop In', which is an outreach to young mothers. Twice a year we have a clothing exchange, when the mothers bring in the clothes their children have grown out of and sell them at very low prices. At the same time they can buy clothes in the next size up, for their children to grow into for the next season. A friend of mine boasts that throughout her children's growing years she regularly bought their entire wardrobe for £5.

Of course it's good to have the occasional treat or special outfit, but by resisting the pressure to conform to every fashion whim we are teaching a much more important lesson. We can prevent our children from picking up the 'designer mentality', which measures people by how well dressed they are and by what they have instead of who they are.

Older children, and particularly young teenage girls, might enjoy having a 'swap' party (with their parents' permission), where they can exchange clothes they have worn once and grown bored with.

Taking responsibility

As parents we are the most important influence in our children's lives. Later on, in their teens, the opinions and fashions of their friends and peer groups play a large part in their thinking, but it is the attitudes and values they absorb in their formative years which govern the principles on which they build their lives. It's the day-to-day minutiae of everyday life that build these principles – not occasional lectures on morality. It's the time, affection and care we give our children, when they have the opportunity to observe how we respond to them and to other people, which help them to learn respect, love, self-discipline and unselfishness.

This is a great challenge to us as parents. Our own example has much more effect than any amount of instruction, because it's absorbed unconsciously. Habits are more easily caught than taught. Just as children imitate our speech patterns and even facial expressions, they pick up the way we welcome people into our homes, or the way we plan our activities. It means we have to discipline ourselves to set the examples we want them to see, biting back irritated retorts or ungenerous statements.

In the same way, their feelings of self-worth will be influenced by the way we view the shape of our bodies, and their future attitudes to diet and health will be affected by our eating habits. Mark Greene, Director of the London Institute for Contemporary Christianity, says, 'The majority of girls are living with adult women who do not like their bodies much and who are constantly concerned about their weight. They're called "Mum".' In a survey, 92 per cent of readers of *Bliss* magazine (for early teens) were unhappy with the way they looked.

> '*Education is what survives when what you learned has been forgotten.*'
>
> *James Jones*

Choosing your battles

Children grow up quickly. There seems to be only a brief lull between toddler tantrums and teenage troubles, and a standard cause of irritation is the state of their bedrooms. Sometimes it seems that whenever they ask if they can do something, your reply is, 'Not until you've tidied your room!' Rob Parsons said that whenever he went into his teenage son's room he used to look up and remark, 'My, you've got a tidy ceiling!' There's a man who believes in being positive.

Is it worth fighting battles about the state of their rooms? Or is the mess actually an assertion of their growing independence? It may be a form of mild rebellion that we would prefer to some of the alternatives. If we're going to have conflicts with our teenagers, it may be an idea to save our arguments for the battles that matter. My mother used to say, 'Choose the mountain you want to die on!'

It's important to define which qualities we really want to encourage in our children. If pressed, most of us would agree that thoughtfulness, honesty and kindness are ultimately more important than tidiness. We'd prefer a messy, dependable friend to a tidy but uncaring one. It's easier to work on encouraging these qualities if our relationship hasn't already become a one-issue battleground. Let's focus on the important things rather than on the unimportant ones – and give our children a sense of proportion at the same time.

Psalm 32 contains a message which I found very helpful: 'I will guide you along the best pathway for your life. I will advise you and watch over you' (Psalm 32:8). Recognising that God had a plan for my life meant also acknowledging that he knew the best path for my children. It released me from the pressure to conform to society's demands for children to be clever or successful. They were his children, too, and he would guide them as well as me.

What really constitutes success for our children? Would we place a higher value on academic achievement, a high-flying career, or generosity of spirit and a love of the Lord?

What empty nest?

Evangelism has always been close to my heart, and for over 25 years I have been involved with an organisation called Activate, which resources and inspires people to take part in low-key evangelism among their friends and neighbours. As the children grew up I was able to take on more work, such as speaking engagements. Roy once said to me, 'I'm really glad that you've found a focus in your life before the children leave home. It means you'll never suffer from empty nest syndrome.'

I was grateful for that encouragement when the children finally did move away. I saw so many people (especially mothers) who were adrift when their children left. They hadn't maintained their relationship with their spouse, or with their friends, and they had no central activity to interest them. I realised how important it was for me to have something that made my life feel purposeful – and even more so after Roy died. I needed a reason to get up in the morning, and the work of reaching out with the love of Christ gave me just that.

All this may seem a long way from decluttering our children's rooms, but it is a part of looking at our attitude to our children and their attitude to us. Just as we want our children to grow up to be independent of us, we must also make sure that we don't become too dependent on them.

However, our empty nest may still contain our children's clutter. Quite often they leave home but their stuff doesn't! I have a 30-something daughter who has left home, but her things haven't followed her. I gently suggest that she takes away a drawer-full every time she comes to visit me, and she thinks it's a very good idea – but she hasn't done it yet. Perhaps I'm not firm enough.

Some young people don't manage to leave home at all, or they go off to university and then come home again, because it's cheaper and more convenient to live there. That's no problem, as long as the family can adapt to living together as adults, instead of as adults and children.

If you are a young adult living at home with your parents, perhaps you should take stock of your situation. For instance, do you demand to be treated as an adult in all respects but fail to take a share of the responsibility for the home? Do you make a financial contribution? Do you do your share of the household tasks? Do you respect your parents by letting them know your movements? They may no longer have authority over you, but you know quite well that they'll still worry if you're late home.

We all know how hard it is for young people to find affordable housing these days, but look at your conscience. Are you exploiting your parents financially, emotionally or physically by letting them go on looking after you willingly and lovingly? What is that doing to the balance of your relationship with them, and to your view of yourself as a mature adult?

Taking Action

Parenting: www.readtogether.co.uk;
www.mediafamily.org

Stop and Think

'What's really important to you? What would you go to the mat for? Some of the qualities that we hold high in our home are self-control, kindness, courtesy, honesty, hard work, generosity, respect. Don't spin your wheels on the unimportant things – save your energy for the important issues.'

Jani Ortlund

The Attic

12

Releasing the Past

It may not be an attic, of course, it may be a cellar or a garage, but you know the area we're in – the general dumping ground. These are the clutter centres. It's so easy to put things in the loft and forget about them (until the bedroom ceiling falls in). When I was a child, we had a cellar which was the home for everything: tools, mowers, plant pots, bits of wood, old suitcases, cardboard boxes. It didn't matter whether something worked or not, or whether the thing would ever be used again – it had a home in the cellar.

My husband Roy was a hoarder. He wouldn't throw anything away in case it would 'come in handy'. I think it came from growing up during the war, when 'waste not, want not' was the order of the day. Early habits of frugality die hard, and of course being frugal and reusing things is very much what we're trying to encourage today, with our emphasis on recycling. The trouble in Roy's case was that though he always said 'It might come in handy', it never did. Whenever he needed something, he went out and bought it new, because he could never put his hand on the old one in the jumble of all the things he was keeping.

When he died we had to get rid of all the props and costumes he had been hoarding for years. We filled an entire skip with all the rubbish, and I said to the children, 'If Dad had taken my advice we wouldn't be having to do this.' My daughter looked up to the sky and said, 'Yes, but guess who's getting the last laugh!'

I'm the opposite; I'm a chucker. I remember the day I was moving house, two years after Roy died. I was wandering around taking a last rather wistful and nostalgic look at the home where our children grew up. Then the Lord spoke into my heart the words of Jesus: 'Anyone who puts a hand to the plough and then looks back is not fit for the Kingdom of God' (Luke 9:62). That was enough. I thanked him for all my happy memories and moved forward into the next part of my life's adventure.

I've cleared out everything of mine from my attic, apart from two suitcases. I really don't need anything more than that. But my children's things are still up there, and they show no signs of removing them, even though they themselves left home years ago. Still, when I die and they want to clear the house and sell it, at least it will only be their own things they're clearing!

Elephants' graveyard

Is your attic the last resting place of obscure bits of equipment, a sorry record of abandoned projects and failed hobbies? Is it full of unfinished tapestries, pieces of wood for the bird table you never got round to making, unused sewing machines, dress fabrics, golf clubs or running shoes? And while we're on the subject, did you take out a gym subscription in January and stop going in March?

When you're decluttering the attic, you may decide to get rid of some of these things by taking them to the charity shop. Or you may decide you really want to have another attempt at whatever activity they represent, whether it's being creative, DIY or getting fit. On the spiritual level you may want to ask yourself why it's so easy to take up a hobby, and to enjoy the interest and excitement of buying the equipment and visualising yourself as slim and energetic, or successfully making a new career selling home-made candles at the craft fair . . . and why it's so hard to keep at it, when the weather makes going out less than inviting, or your first attempts at candle-making are wobbly and misshapen.

Rod Laver, the tennis star, once said, 'People are always telling me how lucky I am to be so successful. And I always say that it's a funny thing – the harder I work, the luckier I become!' Success in any venture demands dedication, hard work, discipline and single-mindedness. 'Remember that in a race everyone runs, but only one person gets the prize. You must also run in such a way that you will win . . . I discipline my body like an athlete, training it to do what it should' (1 Corinthians 9:24, 27). Successful people never give up. If they fail, they get up again and get going, learning from their mistakes. Many people who fail do so only because they give up trying.

When Paul likened himself to an athlete training for a competition, he was thinking of the challenges of the spiritual life. Following Christ is costly, for we have to give up our commitment to our own selfish desires, and focus instead on living the Christ-like life, handing over the lordship of our lives to God. 'You cannot be my disciple if you do not carry your own cross and follow me. But don't begin until you count the cost' (Luke 14:27–28). We know from experience that even if we think we have counted the cost and made our commitment, sometimes the bills that come in are bigger than we expected. Being a Christian may be costly in terms of time, money and energy. It can be very tempting to give in, to say, 'I didn't realise it would be this hard,' and to go back to our old, easy life of pleasing ourselves. Yet to do so is to turn our back on God.

God himself is always faithful to us; he never lets us down. Let's look hard at our faithfulness to God and offer ourselves wholeheartedly to his service. He will give us the strength to persevere in all our efforts.

The cellar of your soul

The other things we store in our cellars and attics are usually items from the past, things we no longer want or need in our everyday lives. Yet we can't bear to get rid of them – the letters and photographs from past relationships, the pictures and vases we dislike and don't want to display, the broken tools. All these stored items of junk have a parallel in our spiritual decluttering. It's easy to tuck away unresolved issues, the angers, irritations and unforgiven wrongs, until something goes wrong and the ceiling of our relationships falls in. One day you make a sharp retort to an old friend or relation, and you realise that you've been nursing some injury for years and have failed to forgive as fully and freely as you should.

Have a good look around the cellar of your soul and bring what you find there into the light of Christ. It's possible to ignore some of our less worthy thoughts and motives while they're hidden in the darkness, but ask God to show you what you need to recognise. When we clear out the attic and place our junk on the lawn in the sunshine, it looks so scruffy and drab that we wonder why we were keeping it. In the same way, when we bring out our old resentments and hurt feelings and place them beside the love and forgiveness of Jesus, they look mean and tawdry. Let's ask for forgiveness and throw them away.

We can choose to remain as victims of our past problems or we can release them, place them at the foot of the cross and move forward in freedom to the future God has prepared for us. 'Let us strip off every weight that slows us down, especially the sin that so easily hinders our progress. And let us run with endurance the race that God has set before us. We do this by keeping our eyes on Jesus, on whom our faith depends from start to finish' (Hebrews 12:1–2). When we build our life around God's purpose, wrong relationships will die and right ones will be born. We will be able to ignore selfish distractions and pursue our calling single-mindedly, to God's glory.

Taking Action

Tools: www.tfsr.org.uk (tools for self-reliance)

Prayer

Lord Jesus, please look into the dark places in my heart, and show me the clutter I have been hanging on to. Help me to identify, by the clear light of your Spirit, all the distractions that hold me back from seeking your will for me with all my heart. Help me to throw aside all my selfishness, pride and worldliness, and find the perfect freedom of serving you. Amen.

The Garden

13
The Glory of Creation

I'm not a gardener. My ideal garden would be a tiny paved courtyard with a plant pot in each corner, filled with silk flowers that I could wash once a week. No weeding, no planting, no pruning. My neighbour has a beautiful garden, and I'm sure he's always looking over at my weedy patch and thinking of all the weed seeds that are floating across the road onto his lawn. That does worry me a bit.

Roy was a brilliant gardener, growing flowers and shrubs and vegetables. He loved to tend his garden; he found it relaxing and a wonderful place to pray. A year after he died, the garden had become a wilderness, because I simply didn't have the time to devote to it and I didn't enjoy gardening as he did.

Do you worry about your neighbours like I worry about mine? Are you concerned in case your scruffy front garden is letting the street down? If your garden is the pride of the area, does it govern your life with its demands? Perhaps you feel it's important that you have the latest paving, or water feature, or exotic plant in order to keep up with the Joneses next door.

Gardening is lovely if it serves you and helps you relax. Wise people don't just schedule appointments in their diaries – they schedule down-time, too. When you're engaged in decluttering your life, make sure you don't become so anxious and driven that you have to be doing good works every second of your day. That way lies burnout. Take some time for yourself to enjoy whatever gift God has given you for that purpose. It may be gardening, or it may be playing or listening to music, or sitting down with a good book. Whatever it is, give thanks for the opportunity, and refresh yourself for God's service.

Perhaps you don't have a garden and wish you had. Make your way to your nearest park and thank God for its peace and beauty and that you don't have to contribute to its upkeep!

My son Daniel has just taken on an allotment and extols its virtues. It costs him very little (he rents from the local council). He benefits from being outside in the fresh air and getting some exercise; he can teach his children about growing things and they can share in the fun; and they can grow healthy, fresh, organic produce at a fraction of the price they would pay at the supermarket.

Down to earth

There are ways of living simply in the garden, too, if you do a bit of research. It isn't necessary to spend the earth on bedding plants when seeds are so cheap. Some people club together to buy seeds when their gardens are so small that they never use a whole packet. If you have a greenhouse, perhaps you could bring on trays of seedlings to share with your neighbours.

Gardeners are often very generous, and will let you take cuttings from their shrubs or even propagate them for you. Church fêtes, school fairs and Women's Institute markets are all excellent places to buy plants and you will also be supporting a good cause.

If you feel that you must keep your garden in reasonable condition, but don't want to spend the time on it, there are plenty of planting schemes which don't require too much effort. Any of your gardening friends will be happy to advise you about low-maintenance plants and shrubs.

Have a look in your garden shed, too, and get rid of things that could help someone else. They may be only old spades, rakes or trowels to you, but they could be useful to an urban garden project or an allotment association, helping volunteers to improve their local environment. Good stewardship of time, money and goods is a service we owe to God; let's be as aware as we can of our own actions and how they can benefit others.

Growing your own

One of the jobs I do enjoy in the garden is sweeping leaves. I suppose this is because I tend to treat my garden the way I treat my house. I clean it and tidy it and not much more. In other words, I'm not a bit creative!

I remember a day long ago when I was driving somewhere to speak at a meeting. I was still quite a young Christian and I was terribly nervous. It was a sunny autumn day, and as I drove along I saw a man sweeping fallen leaves from his lawn. I was so envious. 'It's all right for you,' I thought. 'You can be out here in the sunshine and the autumn colours. I've got to go and face this meeting and speak in public. I'd much rather be sweeping leaves.'

Then a little voice inside me spoke up: 'But if you were sweeping leaves you wouldn't have the opportunity to tell people about Jesus!' It was a turning point for me. I knew I wouldn't give up that privilege for anything.

What does God want you to spend your creative energies on? It may be growing your own vegetables; it may be glorying in his creation (a garden is a good place to think and pray). It may be using your garden as a focus for some outreach activity (inviting your neighbours for a barbecue, or offering a friend a cup of tea and an hour of peace).

Whatever it is, God will have planted the seeds for it in your life already. All you have to do is recognise those seedlings as the opportunities they are, and nurture them accordingly. Learn to use what you have to his glory, in every part of your life.

Taking Action

Low-maintenance gardening: www.bbc.co.uk/gardening

Prayer

Father, thank you for creating and giving us this wonderful world to be our home. Open my eyes to see the beauty of your creation, and my heart to feel the wonder of your love. Help me to use my energy and creativity to honour you and do your will. In Jesus' name. Amen.

The Back Door

14
Tackling Physical Clutter

Decluttering is trendy. There are books and television programmes dedicated to showing people how to tidy up their homes and get rid of things they've been keeping for years. Quite often, the people involved come to realise that their 'clutter' represents something much deeper in their lives than just a few holiday souvenirs they've never got round to throwing away. Clinging on to possessions can be a sign of a buried awareness of failed relationships or unfulfilled dreams. Impulse-buying can be a symptom of emptiness, an attempt to fill a need we haven't acknowledged. For Christians, identifying these emotional and spiritual needs can send us back to our heavenly Father to ask for help and the fulfilling power of the Holy Spirit.

Getting rid of clutter helps us to have a clear vision and peace in our hearts. We may dismiss the New Age spirituality of feng shui, but still acknowledge the energy that comes from living simply. When we combine this with willing discipleship, it enables us to follow Jesus more wholeheartedly. We're getting rid of distractions, opening a channel and releasing the power of the Holy Spirit into our lives.

Let's have a brief look at the issue of dealing with physical clutter.

The problem . . . and what it does to you

- Clutter takes up physical space . . . so you feel crowded, hemmed in by your home.
- Clutter takes up mental space . . . so you feel oppressed by your possessions, which demand storage, cleaning, insurance, etc.
- Clutter makes it difficult to tidy or clean . . . so you feel as if your home is out of control.
- Clutter makes it hard to find things you need . . . so you waste time hunting for bills, papers, your keys.
- Clutter looks messy and is visually distracting . . . so you feel unable to concentrate.
- Clutter represents activities and events that are no longer part of your life . . . so you feel bogged down in the past and unable to move on.

Assessing the problem

First of all, let's assess the scale of the problem. Give your home a clutter rating: in the box below, make a mark on each line somewhere between the two extremes. That should establish which areas need priority attention.

Hall

A welcoming entrance . . . . Obstacle course

Living room

Calm, relaxing haven . . . . Clear a chair to sit down

Kitchen

Ready for action . . . . No room to chop an apple

Dining room

Family meal time . . . . Shrine to occasional banquets

Bathroom

Clean and calming. . . . . Pharmaceutical graveyard

Study

Efficiency reigns . . . . Raiders of the Lost Archive

Bedroom

Ready for rest . . . . The floor is my laundry basket

Children's rooms

A place to play . . . . Toys R Everywhere

Attic/garage/cellar

Neat and tidy . . . . Scrapheap challenge

Garden

A place to relax . . . . A walk in the wilderness

So where do we go from here? There are four stages in tackling your physical clutter: identify it; sort it; deal with it; and avoid it in the future.

Identify it

Everything in your home should earn its place there by being useful or by giving you pleasure. Anything you don't really want, need or use is just clutter.

It's fairly easy to identify what is useful. Ask yourself this question: have I used this item in the last year? Most things will be in regular use more often than that, but allowing a year gives us a wide margin (and leaves us the Christmas decorations).

What about giving pleasure? We need to exercise a little self-control here, or we can get swamped by items we like the look of. Ask yourself: when did I last really look at and appreciate this item? If you can't remember, it probably doesn't mean that much to you. But if that wobbly clay sculpture made by your five-year-old makes you smile every time you dust it, then it earns its keep. If you have been given something by a friend and looking at it reminds you to pray for that person, or get in touch with them, then it's proving its value.

Sort it

When you declutter a room, aim to clear every surface. Equip yourself with some large cardboard boxes and label them as follows:

- *Essential.* Items you use all the time or love for their decorative or sentimental value.
- *Rubbish.* This is for used envelopes, old catalogues and coupons, unused make-up, and that single screw that came out of something six months ago.
- *Broken.* Useful items which genuinely need repair.
- *Charity.* These are items you don't love or need, but which are in good condition. Take them to the charity shop and let someone else benefit from them.
- *Nostalgia.* These are the things you really want to keep: your wedding dress, a child's first school blazer, a special invitation, programme or greetings card.

Deal with it

You don't want to trip over five large cardboard boxes for a week, so make sure you deal with it all.

- *Essential.* Don't just put these items back – you may find that they look better in another room or another location once you've finished clearing. Think laterally about storage solutions. Do you need a magazine rack? Could you get small containers for door keys, remote controls, window locks, radiator keys, or anything else you regularly waste time hunting for?
- *Rubbish.* Obviously, put it in the dustbin, take it to the tip, or put it in the recycling bin.
- *Broken.* How long has it been broken? Can you get it repaired this week? If it isn't that urgent, do you really need it?

- *Charity*. Whether the items in this box are clothes, magazines, books or jumble, make sure they leave the house and get to the charity shop or jumble sale.
- *Nostalgia*. Be strict with yourself here, and set a limit on how much you can keep. Ask yourself why you want to keep things. Are you stuck in the past for any reason? For things you really want to keep, there are two good techniques. First, *miniaturise*: keep a swatch of fabric, not the whole dress; cut the badge or a button off the blazer. Then, *display*: if you really want to keep these memories, enjoy them. Put together a display – a pressed flower, your fabric, an invitation and a wedding photo – and frame it.

I confess that I kept my own wedding dress for years – mainly out of pride that I could still get into it. I used to try it on every five years to check! Then I met someone who made beautiful fabric pictures, so I gave it to her to use as she chose. Among the lovely things she made from it was a picture of a little girl, which she gave to me. Now I can enjoy both my nostalgia and my friend's creativity.

Avoid it

I realise now that my mother had her own methods of avoiding clutter. Her standard sayings were: 'Don't put it down, put it away' (it taught us to be tidy); 'If not now, when?' (an excellent antidote to the 'I'll do it later' excuse we all hide behind); and 'When you say "That'll do", it probably won't' (how often do we leave a job half done, so that it continues to irritate us?). Bear these in mind, and once you've cleared your clutter, keep it down. Practise some techniques for preventing clutter from taking over again.

- *One touch*. Make sure you handle papers only once: file your bank statement when it arrives – don't put it in a huge filing pile that you'll get round to one day. Pay bills when they arrive, or place them in your desk diary for the day they must be paid. Write important dates (and *all* the details) into your diary and dispose of the letter, flyer or card which gave you the information.
- *One in, one out*. If you buy a new book, look critically at your bookshelf and see if there's a book you're unlikely to read again. Take it to the charity shop the next time you're passing.
- *Queue here*. If you're downstairs, and you have an item that should be upstairs, place it by the foot of the stairs (*not* where you'll fall over it). It is now waiting at the bus stop. Take it with you the next time you go upstairs; don't leave it until there's a pile of things. And when you get upstairs, make sure you put it away.

What we focus on becomes the dominating force in our lives. Whatever gets your attention, gets you.

Our tour of the house has also been a tour of our Christian lives. Looking at some of the physical items that fill our homes and absorb our time, energy and attention, we can be alerted to our real priorities and preoccupations. Is there a parallel between dealing with physical clutter and avoiding spiritual clutter? What techniques can we use to keep ourselves from slipping back into those worldly attitudes and unthinking habits? Let's make a resolution to pay attention to God's will through our reading of the Bible, and by asking for his guidance and strength in prayer. Then we can begin to simplify our lives to make space for God.

15

Help Is at Hand

If you have been praying and thinking about the amount of clutter in your home, you may have come to some conclusions about the amount of clutter in your spiritual life. It can be painful and alarming to become aware of some of our deeper motivations. Here are some scriptures to remind us that God knows us better than we know ourselves – and he still loves us!

1. Do you hoard things because you are afraid of not having enough? Because you are anxious about the future?

- 'God will generously provide all you need. Then you will always have everything you need and plenty left over to share with others' (2 Corinthians 9:8).
- 'To those who use well what they are given, even more will be given, and they will have an abundance' (Matthew 25:29).
- '"For I know the plans I have for you," says the LORD. "They are plans for good and not for disaster, to give you a future and a hope"' (Jeremiah 29:11).

- 'So I tell you, don't worry about everyday life – whether you have enough food, drink and clothes. Doesn't life consist of more than food and clothing?' (Matthew 6:25).

2. Do you display books on your bookshelves to show people how interesting/intelligent/well read you are?

- 'The LORD doesn't make decisions the way you do! People judge by outward appearance, but the LORD looks at a person's thoughts and intentions' (1 Samuel 16:7).
- 'LORD, you have examined my heart and know everything about me . . . How precious are your thoughts about me, O God' (Psalm 139:1, 17).
- 'If you need wisdom – if you want to know what God wants you to do – ask him, and he will gladly tell you' (James 1:5).

3. Do you collect many possessions as a sign of achievement to boost your self-esteem?

- 'See how much our heavenly Father loves us, for he allows us to be called his children' (1 John 3:1).
- 'God has given gifts to each of you from his great variety of spiritual gifts. Manage them well so that God's generosity can flow through you' (1 Peter 4:10).
- 'Don't be concerned about the outward beauty that depends on fancy hairstyles, expensive jewellery or beautiful clothes. You should be known for the beauty that comes from within, the unfading beauty of a gentle and quiet spirit, which is so precious to God' (1 Peter 3:3–4).

4. Do you keep symbols of happy past events because you're afraid of being unhappy now or in the future?

- 'Don't worry about anything; instead, pray about everything . . . If you do this, you will experience God's peace, which is far more wonderful than the human mind can understand' (Philippians 4:6–7).
- 'Give all your worries and cares to God, for he cares about what happens to you' (1 Peter 5:7).
- 'I know the LORD is always with me. I will not be shaken, for he is right beside me. No wonder my mouth is filled with joy, and my mouth shouts his praises' (Psalm 16:8–9).

5. Do you keep things you plan to use but never get round to?

- 'Work hard and cheerfully at whatever you do, as though you were working for the LORD rather than for people' (Colossians 3:23).
- 'With God's help we can do mighty things' (Psalm 60:12).
- 'Those who wait on the LORD will find new strength. They will fly high on wings like eagles. They will run and not grow weary. They will walk and not faint' (Isaiah 40:31).

6. Do you sometimes feel guilty about your standard of living, or about having fun, when there is so much poverty in the world?

- 'Go and celebrate with a feast of choice foods and sweet drinks, and share gifts of food with people who have nothing prepared. This is a sacred day before the LORD. Don't be dejected and sad, for the joy of the LORD is your strength!' (Nehemiah 8:10).

- 'And get into the habit of inviting guests home for dinner or, if they need lodging, for the night' (Romans 12:13).
- 'I want you to share your food with the hungry and to welcome poor wanderers into your homes. Give clothes to those who need them, and do not hide from relatives who need your help' (Isaiah 58:7).

7. Do you often feel that you would be happier if you had a better home, clothes or possessions?

- 'Why spend your money on food that does not give you strength? Why pay money for food that does you no good? Listen, and I will tell you where to get food for the soul' (Isaiah 55:2–3).
- 'I have learned how to get along happily whether I have much or little. I know how to live on almost nothing or with everything . . . For I can do everything with the help of Christ who gives me the strength I need' (Philippians 4:11–13).
- 'True religion with contentment is great wealth. After all, we didn't bring anything with us when we came into the world, and we certainly cannot carry anything with us when we die'(1 Timothy 6:6–7).

16

Living Without Regrets

In this book we have been looking at the things which may have crept into our Christian lives and prevented us from pursuing our destiny: the clutter which deflects us from our primary purpose of finding God's will for us. 'Our aim is to please him always. For we must all stand before Christ and be judged' (2 Corinthians 5:9–10). We know that our salvation is assured through the loving sacrifice of Christ, and our response to the generosity of that love is to want to live our lives in a way that is pleasing to him.

Yet we get bogged down by the circumstances of our everyday lives; we make mistakes, and over and over again we have to turn back to our heavenly Father in penitence and faith, asking for forgiveness. Too often we have regrets about the way we are living our lives. We may regret doing or saying things we wish we hadn't, or we may regret not doing things we wish we had.

It's often the impulsive words and actions which we have scarcely thought about that occasion our regrets. They say that the second half of a person's life is made up of habits he acquired in the first half, and our behaviour, attitudes and choices will largely spring out of these. How can we discipline ourselves to develop godly habits of thought and action, and thus grow in integrity?

As for the things we wish we had done, our failure to act may spring from a lack of faith and not having the confidence to tackle something new or challenging. How can we avoid regretting the things that might have been?

The importance of integrity

When I was struggling in my life as a new Christian, I discovered that God had given me a lively conscience, and I became aware that I was falling short of my own aims. I was always confessing the times I had spoken sharply to someone, or covered up my own actions with some white lie or small deception. I studied the Bible for examples of Christian behaviour, and realised that the Scriptures and prayer were my best teachers. If I could walk every day with Jesus as my example, he would show me the way. But I had to practise this consistently.

My husband Roy was another good example for me. Although his work as an entertainer was unusual, the rest of his life was ordinary. He was a humble family man, yet he was known for his integrity. If Roy said he'd do something, you knew he would never let you down. You could trust him completely. What you saw on television – the cheerful good humour, the honesty, the care for other people – was simply what he was like all the time.

It takes constant vigilance and self-discipline to develop

integrity, never allowing ourselves any latitude for 'small' slips. 'Character is made in the small moments of our lives.' It means constantly being so aware of other people and their needs that we can't say anything hurtful; it means constantly being so aware of God's goodness to us that we can't act meanly towards anyone else; so that we can't lie, or cheat, or gossip without knowing that we aren't living up to God's standards.

They say that if you do something regularly for three weeks you can create a habit. Let's work at creating the habits of integrity.

The might-have-beens

I once heard a couple of lines of a poem which stuck in my head: 'Of all the sorry words of tongue and pen, the saddest ones are these – it might have been.' The things we fail to do may cause us the greatest regrets.

When I started my career on the stage, my father, who had never seemed at all convinced about my dancing, told me to go ahead and 'have the courage to do the things you want to do'. He said there were things he now regretted not doing in his life. I was shocked. He was a wonderful doctor who gave himself unstintingly to his patients. It had never occurred to me that he might have regrets or unfulfilled dreams.

I thought of his words again two days after Roy died. I was invited to give an interview on GMTV, but I had never done an interview without Roy, and I was sure I would get muddled and incoherent. I was terrified that I would fail.

I took it to the Lord in prayer, and God showed me that I should rise to the challenge. 'But what if I mess it up?' I wailed. 'Well, you won't be asked again,' came the answer. I realised that my fear of failing was actually a form of pride. I couldn't bear to look a fool. Well, what did it matter? I swallowed my fear of ridicule, just did it and managed a reasonable performance.

Rising to the challenge in spite of one's fears seems to be a key.

Theodore Roosevelt said:

> The credit belongs to the man who is actually in the arena, whose face is marred by dust and sweat and blood; who . . . spends himself in a worthy cause; who, at best, knows the triumph of high achievement; and who, at worst, if he fails, at least fails while daring greatly, so that his place shall never be with those cold and timid souls who know neither victory nor defeat.

The starfish thrower

I also realised that I didn't want to get to the end of my life and have God say to me, 'Where were you when I needed you? I gave you all these opportunities and you didn't take them. You could have made a difference, but you didn't bother.' I might have felt inadequate and insignificant, but I wanted at least to have tried, and not to look back on the might-have-beens.

I love the story of the little boy who went to the beach one morning after a great storm. Thousands of starfish had been washed up and now lay stranded above the waterline, so he began hurrying along the sand, picking them up and throwing them back into the sea. His father asked him what he was doing.

'I'm trying to save the starfish. If they stay out of the water, they'll die.'

'There's no point,' said his father. 'Look how many there are! Nothing you do can make a difference.'

The little boy looked down at the starfish in his hand, then he threw it out to sea. 'I've made a difference to that one,' he said.

God loves to use the things we think of as insignificant, when he does his work in us. He used a packed lunch to feed five thousand people; a sling and a stone to kill a giant; and a fingerful of mud to restore someone's sight. We may never see the fruits of our work in others – the person we made time for, the child we taught, the neighbour we helped – but they are visible from eternity, shining as pin-pricks of light in a dark world.

The only real requirement is that we should ask God to show us the work he has for us, listen to the answer, and then step out in faith. It is our willingness to do his will, whatever that may be for us, which ensures that we pursue our destiny as God's children.

If you would like to rededicate your life to God's will, you might like to pray the following prayer. From the earliest days of the Methodist Societies, John Wesley invited the people to renew their covenant relationship with God, and Covenant services are still held in Methodist churches every year. This prayer forms part of the act of dedication.

The Methodist Covenant Prayer

I am no longer my own but yours.
Put me to what you will,
rank me with whom you will;
put me to doing, put me to suffering;
let me be employed for you or laid aside for you,
exalted for you or brought low for you;
let me be full, let me be empty,
let me have all things, let me have nothing;
I freely and wholeheartedly yield all things to your
   pleasure and disposal.
And now, glorious and blessed God,
Father, Son and Holy Spirit,
you are mine and I am yours.
So be it.
And the covenant made on earth,
let it be ratified in heaven. Amen.